Egg & Cheese Dishes

Mary Cadogan
Barbara Logan

Cheddar fries with spicy sauce

Preparation time: 15 minutes, plus chilling
Cooking time: 15 minutes

225 g/8 oz Cheddar cheese, cut into 1 cm/½ inch cubes

1 egg, beaten

100 g/4 oz brown breadcrumbs

oil for deep frying

salt

Sauce:

2 teaspoons oil

1 small onion, peeled and chopped

150 ml/¼ pint tomato ketchup

1 tablespoon Worcestershire sauce

2 tablespoons clear honey

2 tablespoons vinegar

1. Coat the cheese cubes in the beaten egg and breadcrumbs twice. Chill while making the sauce.
2. Heat the oil in a small saucepan and gently fry the onion for about 5 minutes until soft.
3. Add the remaining sauce ingredients. Simmer for 5 minutes until thickened.
4. Heat the oil to 180°C/350°F. Fry the cheese cubes, in 2 or 3 batches, for about 2 minutes until golden. Drain well on paper towels.
5. Sprinkle the fries with salt and serve with the spicy sauce.

Cheshire onion soup

Preparation time: 10 minutes
Cooking time: 20 minutes

175 g/6 oz Cheshire cheese

25 g/1 oz butter

1 large onion, peeled and thinly sliced

25 g/1 oz plain flour

300 ml/½ pint stock

450 ml/¾ pint milk

1 teaspoon made English mustard

salt

freshly ground black pepper

1 tablespoon chopped fresh parsley

1. Crumble the cheese between the fingers on to a plate.
2. Melt the butter in a large saucepan and gently fry the onion until soft and lightly browned.
3. Add the flour and cook, stirring, for 1 minute.
4. Gradually stir in the stock and milk. Bring to the boil, stirring until thickened and smooth.
5. Add the mustard, salt and pepper. Simmer for 10 minutes, stirring occasionally.
6. Stir in the cheese and parsley. Heat gently until the cheese has just melted, about 2 minutes. Serve immediately with crusty bread or toast.

Egg & tuna mousse

**Serves 4 as a main course or 8 as a
starter**
Preparation time: 30 minutes
Cooking time: 10 minutes

1 x 275 g/10 oz can asparagus
  pieces

3 teaspoons gelatine

150 ml/¼ pint soured cream

3 tablespoons Mayonnaise
  (card 22)

2 tablespoons chopped onion

3 eggs, hard-boiled, shelled and
  chopped

1 teaspoon curry powder

1 x 200 g/7 oz.can tuna, drained
  and flaked

salt

freshly ground black pepper

1 egg white

To garnish:

cress

paprika

lettuce

stuffed olives

1. Drain the asparagus reserving
4 tablespoons of the liquid.
2. Sprinkle the gelatine over the reserved
liquid in a small heatproof bowl, then leave
until spongy. Stand the bowl in a pan of hot
water and heat gently until the gelatine has
dissolved, stirring occasionally.
3. In a basin mix together the soured
cream, asparagus pieces, mayonnaise,
onion, eggs, curry powder, tuna, salt and
pepper.
4. Stir in the dissolved gelatine.
5. Whisk the egg white until stiff and fold
into the mixture.
6. Pour into individual dishes or a fish
shaped mould and leave to set.
7. Garnish individual mousses with cress
and a sprinkling of paprika.
8. If using a mould turn the mousse out on
to a bed of lettuce and garnish with cress
and olives.
9. Serve as a starter with melba toast or as
a light meal with a salad and rolls.

Cheese & olive sablés

Makes about 20
Preparation time: 20 minutes, plus chilling
Cooking time: 15 minutes
Oven: 200°C, 400°F, Gas Mark 6

75 g/3 oz plain flour

pinch of salt

cayenne pepper

75 g/3 oz butter

25 g/1 oz Parmesan cheese, grated

50 g/2 oz Cheddar cheese, grated

about 20 stuffed olives

1. Place the flour, salt and a good pinch of cayenne pepper in a bowl. Add the butter, cut into small pieces, and rub into the flour with the fingertips.
2. Add the cheeses and draw the mixture together with the fingers to form a firm dough.
3. Turn out on to a floured surface and knead lightly until smooth.
4. Flatten a small piece of dough in the palm of the hand. Place an olive in the centre and bring the dough around the olive to enclose it.
5. Repeat with the remaining dough and olives. Chill for 30 minutes.
6. Place a little apart, on a baking sheet. Place in a preheated oven and bake for about 15 minutes until golden. Serve warm.

Cheese straws

Makes about 80
Preparation time: 15 minutes, plus chilling
Cooking time: 10-15 minutes
Oven: 200°C, 400°F, Gas Mark 6

175 g/6 oz plain flour

salt

2 teaspoons mustard powder

100 g/4 oz butter

50 g/2 oz Cheddar cheese, grated

25 g/1 oz Parmesan cheese, grated

1 egg, beaten

celery or poppy seeds

1. Place the flour, salt and mustard in a bowl. Add the butter, cut into small pieces, and rub in to the flour with the fingertips until the mixture resembles fine breadcrumbs.
2. Add the cheeses and mix well.
3. Add 2 tablespoons beaten egg and mix to form a firm dough.
4. Wrap the dough in cling film and chill for 10 minutes.
5. Roll out the dough and cut into lengths 7.5 cm/3 inches wide. Cut each length into 1 cm/½ inch strips.
6. Twist each strip and place on baking sheets. Brush with the remaining beaten egg and sprinkle with celery seeds or poppy seeds.
7. Place in a preheated oven and bake for 10-15 minutes until crisp and golden. Cool on a wire tray. Serve warm or cold.

Roquefort & walnut toast

Preparation time: 5 minutes
Cooking time: 2 minutes

1 large slice bread

butter

50 g/2 oz Roquefort cheese,
  crumbled

2 teaspoons chopped walnuts

1 teaspoon chopped fresh
  parsley

1. Toast the bread and spread with butter.
2. Sprinkle over the Roquefort cheese and walnuts. Place under a preheated grill until the cheese has melted.
3. Sprinkle with chopped parsley and cut into squares or fingers.

Blue cheese bites

Makes 40
Preparation time: 15 minutes

25 g/1 oz unsalted butter,
  softened

75 g/3 oz full fat soft (cream)
  cheese

50 g/2 oz blue cheese, e.g. Stilton
  or Danish blue, grated

freshly ground black pepper

2 tablespoons chopped fresh
  parsley, paprika or 25 g/1 oz
  walnuts, finely chopped

1. Place the butter and full fat soft cheese in a bowl. Beat with a wooden spoon until well mixed.
2. Add the blue cheese and pepper. Beat until well mixed. If the mixture is too soft to handle, chill for 30 minutes.
3. Form the mixture into tiny balls. Roll in the chopped parsley, paprika or walnuts.
4. Serve on cocktail sticks.

Garlic & herb dip

Preparation time: 5 minutes

225 g/8 oz medium fat soft
  (curd) cheese

3 tablespoons milk

1 tablespoon chopped fresh
  herbs, e.g. parsley, oregano,
  mint

1 garlic clove, peeled and
  crushed

salt

freshly ground black pepper

1. Place the cheese in a bowl. Beat in the milk gradually until smooth.
2. Add the herbs, garlic, salt and pepper. Mix well.
3. Transfer to a serving dish and serve with crisp sticks of raw vegetables, cauliflower florets or savoury crackers.

Onion & cream quiche

Preparation time: 25-30 minutes
Cooking time: 35-40 minutes
Oven: 200°C, 400°F, Gas Mark 6;
    190°C, 375°F, Gas Mark 5

175 g/6 oz plain flour

pinch of salt

75 g/3 oz fat

40 g/1 ½ oz Cheddar cheese,
    grated

pinch of dry mustard

cold water

Filling:

50 g/2 oz butter

450 g/1 lb onions, peeled and
    sliced

3 eggs

200 ml/⅓ pint single cream

salt

freshly ground black pepper

¼ teaspoon dried dill weed

1. Sift the flour and salt into a mixing bowl. Cut the fat into pieces and rub into the flour until the mixture resembles fine breadcrumbs.

2. Add the cheese, mustard and enough cold water to mix to a firm dough. Knead lightly then roll out and use to line a 20 cm/8 inch flan ring placed on a baking sheet.

3. Line with a piece of foil and cook in a preheated oven for 10 minutes.

4. Remove the foil and set the pastry case on one side. Reduce the oven temperature.

5. Melt the butter in a saucepan, add the onion and fry until soft. Put into the pastry case.

6. Beat together the eggs, cream, salt, pepper and dill weed. Pour into the pastry case.

7. Cook in the preheated oven for 25-30 minutes.

8. Serve as a main meal with courgettes and duchesse potatoes.

Variation:
Leek and ham quiche: In place of the onions use sliced leeks and add 100 g/4 oz chopped ham to the filling.

Prawn & egg curry

Preparation time: 25 minutes
Cooking time: 35-40 minutes

3 tablespoons oil

100 g/4 oz onions, peeled and sliced

1 large cooking apple, peeled, cored and chopped

2-3 tablespoons curry powder

1 tablespoon plain flour

1 tablespoon mango chutney

2 teaspoons tomato purée

50 g/2 oz sultanas

1 tablespoon demerara sugar

1 x 300 g/11 oz can pineapple cubes

about 450 ml/¾ pint light stock or water

175 ml/6 fl oz soured cream

175-225 g/6-8 oz peeled prawns

9 eggs, hard-boiled and shelled

225 g/8 oz long-grain rice

To serve:

desiccated coconut

mango chutney

sliced banana in lemon juice

peanuts

poppadoms

1. Heat the oil in a saucepan, add the onion and fry for 5-6 minutes. Add the apple and fry for a further 2-3 minutes.

2. Stir in the curry powder, flour, chutney, tomato purée, sultanas and sugar, and cook for 3-4 minutes.

3. Drain the juice from the can of pineapple and make up to 600 ml/1 pint with the stock or water. Stir the liquid into the saucepan, bring to the boil, cover and simmer for 20-25 minutes.

4. Add the pineapple, reserving a few pieces, the soured cream, prawns and 8 whole eggs. Heat for a further 5 minutes. Slice the remaining egg.

5. Cook the rice in boiling salted water for 12-15 minutes until just cooked, drain and put into a serving dish.

6. Arrange the whole eggs on top and pour the sauce over. Garnish with the sliced egg and remaining pineapple.

7. Serve with individual dishes of coconut, chutney, banana and peanuts and with poppadoms.

Eggs fruits de mer

**Preparation time: 10 minutes
Cooking time: 20 minutes**

50 g/2 oz butter

40 g/1½ oz plain flour

450 ml/¾ pint milk

3 tablespoons single cream

3 tablespoons white wine

2 egg yolks

salt

freshly ground black pepper

8 eggs, hard-boiled, shelled and halved

1 x 75 g/3 oz can smoked oysters

1 x 100 g/4 oz jar baby clams, drained

1 x 150 g/5 oz jar mussels, drained

2 tablespoons browned breadcrumbs

fleurons of puff pastry, to garnish

1. Melt the butter in a saucepan, add the flour and cook for 1-2 minutes.
2. Gradually stir in the milk, and stirring constantly, simmer for 2-3 minutes.
3. Stir in the cream, wine, egg yolks, salt and pepper. Keep the sauce hot but do not allow to boil.
4. Arrange the egg halves in a shallow flameproof dish and add the oysters, clams and mussels.
5. Pour over the sauce, sprinkle with breadcrumbs and place under a preheated hot grill for 2-3 minutes.
6. Garnish with the fleurons, or insert triangles of toast round the edge. Serve with a green salad.

Variation: In place of oysters, clams and mussels use: 1 x 200 g/7 oz can shrimps, drained and 1 x 150 g/5 oz jar cockles, drained.

Eggs with watercress

Serves 4 as a main course or 8 as a starter

2 bunches of watercress

5 tablespoons Mayonnaise (card 22)

salt

freshly ground black pepper

finely grated rind and juice of ½ lemon

8 eggs

paprika

3 tomatoes, sliced

50 g/2 oz onions, peeled and thinly sliced

2 tablespoons French dressing

chopped fresh parsley, to garnish

1. Remove the tough stalks from the watercress, wash well and put into a saucepan. Cover with cold water, bring to the boil, cover and simmer for 10 minutes.
2. Drain well, and chop finely.
3. Mix together the watercress, 3 tablespoons of the mayonnaise, salt, pepper, lemon rind and juice, and spread the mixture over the bottom of a flat plate.
4. Boil the eggs for 5 minutes, shell and arrange them on the watercress.
5. Spoon the remaining mayonnaise over the top of the eggs and sprinkle with paprika.
6. Arrange the sliced tomatoes and onion alternately round the edge of the plate, spoon over the French dressing and sprinkle with parsley. Serve as a light meal, or with melba toast as a starter. This is also good for a buffet.

Cheese & smoked mackerel gougère

Preparation time: 20 minutes
Cooking time: 40 minutes
Oven: 200°C, 400°F, Gas Mark 6

150 ml/¼ pint water

50 g/2 oz butter

65 g/2½ oz plain flour

2 eggs, beaten

pinch of salt

75 g/3 oz Cheddar cheese, grated

Filling:

175 g/6 oz smoked mackerel,
  skinned and flaked

450 g/1 lb tomatoes, skinned and
  chopped

1 tablespoon chopped fresh
  parsley

salt

freshly ground black pepper

25 g/1 oz Cheddar cheese, grated

1. Place the water and butter in a saucepan. Heat until the butter has melted, then bring to the boil.
2. Remove from heat and quickly add the flour, all at once. Beat until the mixture leaves the sides of the pan.
3. Return to the heat and cook for 1 minute. Remove pan from the heat.
4. Cool slightly, then beat in the egg, a little at a time. Stir in the salt and 75 g/3 oz cheese.
5. To make the filling, mix together the mackerel, tomatoes, parsley, salt and pepper.
6. Spread the cheese choux pastry around the edge of a buttered 1.75 litre/3 pint ovenproof dish.
7. Pour the filling in the centre and sprinkle with the cheese.
8. Place in a preheated oven and bake for 35 minutes until risen and golden brown.

Crab & cheese mousse

Preparation time: 20 minutes, plus
chilling

1 x 150 g/5 oz can crab meat,
  drained, reserving juice

100 g/4 oz Cheddar cheese, finely
  grated

150 ml/¼ pint double cream

2 tablespoons tomato ketchup

1 tablespoon lemon juice

salt

pinch of cayenne pepper

15 g/½ oz gelatine

2 egg whites

Garnish:

thin slices of cucumber

sprigs of watercress

1. Place the drained crab meat in a large bowl. Flake with a fork.
2. Add the cheese, cream, ketchup, lemon juice, salt and cayenne pepper. Mix well.
3. Place the reserved juice from the can of crab in a small bowl or cup. Sprinkle with the gelatine. Place in a saucepan of hot water and stir until dissolved.
4. Stir the dissolved gelatine thoroughly into the crab mixture.
5. Whisk the egg whites until stiff. Fold into the crab mixture with a metal spoon, cutting through the mixture until all the egg white is evenly incorporated.
6. Pour the mixture into a wetted 20 cm/8 inch ring mould. Chill for about 2 hours until set.
7. Turn the mould out on to a serving plate. Garnish with the cucumber and watercress.

Steak with Stilton

Preparation time: 10 minutes, plus chilling
Cooking time: 10 minutes

75 g/3 oz Stilton cheese, at room temperature

50 g/2 oz butter, softened

1 tablespoon lemon juice

4 sirloin or rump steaks

oil

freshly ground black pepper

sprigs of watercress, to garnish

1. Crumble the Stilton into a small bowl. Add the butter and lemon juice, and beat together until smooth and well mixed.
2. Place the mixture in a piece of foil or greaseproof paper large enough to completely enclose it. Form into a roll about 2.5 cm/1 inch wide. Wrap and chill for about 1 hour.
3. Rub the steaks with a little oil and sprinkle with pepper.
4. Place the steaks under a preheated hot grill and cook for 2-5 minutes each side, depending on your taste.
5. Serve the steaks on hot plates, topped with overlapping slices of Stilton butter. Garnish with the watercress.

Cheese pilaff

Preparation time: 15 minutes
Cooking time: about 50 minutes
Oven: 180°C, 350°F, Gas Mark 4

50 g/2 oz butter

1 large onion, peeled and sliced

1 red pepper, cored, seeded and sliced

225 g/8 oz courgettes, sliced

225 g/8 oz brown rice, washed and drained

½ teaspoon ground turmeric

½ teaspoon cayenne

1-2 teaspoons salt

freshly ground black pepper

750 ml/1¼ pints hot stock

175 g/6 oz Cheddar cheese, grated

1. Melt the butter in a flameproof casserole and fry the onion for about 5 minutes.
2. Add the red pepper, courgettes, rice, turmeric, cayenne, salt and pepper. Fry for 2 minutes, stirring.
3. Add the hot stock and cover with a well-fitting lid. Place in a preheated oven and cook for 45 minutes until the rice is tender and the stock absorbed.
4. Stir in the cheese until melted and serve hot.

Baked wheatmeal pancakes

Preparation time: 20 minutes
Cooking time: 35 minutes
Oven: 190°C, 375°F, Gas Mark 5

50 g/2 oz wheatmeal flour

salt

50 g/2 oz plain flour

1 egg

300 ml/½ pint milk

oil for shallow frying

Filling:

25 g/1 oz butter

25 g/1 oz plain flour

150 ml/¼ pint milk

salt

freshly ground black pepper

½ teaspoon celery seeds

1 tablespoon chopped fresh parsley

100 g/4 oz cooked ham, cut into small cubes

1 egg, beaten

150 g/5 oz Cheddar cheese, grated

1. Place the wheatmeal flour and salt in a bowl. Sift in the plain flour. Make a well in the centre and add the egg.

2. Beat in the milk gradually, drawing in the flour from the sides, until the batter is smooth and glossy.

3. Heat a little oil in an 18 cm/7 inch frying pan. Pour off the excess.

4. Pour in enough batter to thinly coat the base of the pan. Cook until the underside is golden brown, then turn over with a palette knife to complete cooking.

5. Slide the pancake on to a heated plate and keep warm while making the remaining pancakes. This amount of batter will make 8 pancakes.

6. Melt the butter in a saucepan. Stir in the flour and cook for 1 minute.

7. Remove from the heat and gradually stir in the milk. Add the salt, pepper and celery seeds. Bring to the boil and simmer for 2 minutes, stirring occasionally, until thickened and smooth.

8. Remove from the heat and add the parsley, ham, beaten egg and 100 g/4 oz of the cheese. Stir well.

9. Spread a little filling across the centre of each pancake and roll up. Arrange in a buttered shallow ovenproof dish.

10. Sprinkle with the remaining cheese. Place in a preheated oven and bake for 20 minutes until the cheese topping is golden brown.

Two-cheese pizza

Preparation time: 25 minutes, plus rising
Cooking time: 1 hour
Oven: 200°C, 400°F, Gas Mark 6

150 ml/¼ pint warm water

1 teaspoon sugar

1 teaspoon dried yeast

225 g/8 oz wheatmeal flour

1 teaspoon salt

15 g/½ oz butter

Topping:

1 tablespoon olive oil

1 garlic clove, peeled and crushed

1 onion, peeled and sliced

1 x 400 g/14 oz can tomatoes

2 tablespoons tomato purée

1 teaspoon chopped fresh oregano or ½ teaspoon dried oregano

1 teaspoon brown sugar

salt

freshly ground black pepper

100 g/4 oz Mozzarella cheese, sliced

100 g/4 oz Danish blue or Stilton cheese, sliced

1 tablespoon capers, drained

4 anchovies, drained

10 stuffed olives

1. Measure the water into a jug. Add the sugar and yeast, and leave for 10 minutes until frothy.

2. Place the flour and salt in a bowl. Rub in the butter. Add the yeast liquid all at once and mix to a soft dough.

3. On a floured surface, knead the dough for 5 minutes until smooth and pliable. Place the dough in an oiled polythene bag and leave for about 30 minutes to rise.

4. Meanwhile, to make the topping, heat the oil in a saucepan and gently fry the garlic and onion for about 10 minutes until softened.

5. Add the tomatoes, tomato purée, oregano, sugar, salt and pepper. Bring to the boil and simmer gently for about 20 minutes until thickened. Leave to cool.

6. Roll out the dough to a 30 cm/12 inch round. Place on an oiled baking sheet.

7. Spread the tomato sauce over the dough to within 1 cm/½ inch of the edge.

8. Arrange alternate slices of Mozzarella and blue cheese in triangles around the top of the pizza.

9. Chop the capers and anchovies together. Sprinkle over the pizza. Top with the stuffed olives.

10. Place in a preheated oven and bake for 25-30 minutes until the dough is golden brown and the cheeses have melted.

Cheese soufflé with poached eggs

Preparation time: 20 minutes
Cooking time: 45 minutes
Oven: 200°C, 400°F, Gas Mark 6

6 eggs

50 g/2 oz butter

50 g/2 oz plain flour

300 ml/½ pint milk

salt

freshly ground black pepper

100 g/4 oz Leicester cheese,
  grated

1. Fill a large pan with 2.5 cm/1 inch water. Heat until just simmering.
2. Carefully slide in 4 of the eggs and poach until the whites have just set. Remove from the pan with a slotted spoon and keep warm in a bowl of warm water.
3. Melt the butter in a saucepan. Stir in the flour and cook for 1 minute.
4. Remove from the heat and gradually stir in the milk. Bring to the boil and simmer for 2 minutes, stirring occasionally, until thickened and smooth.
5. Separate the remaining 2 eggs. Remove the sauce from the heat and beat in the salt, pepper, egg yolks and cheese.
6. Whisk the egg whites until stiff. Fold into the cheese mixture with a metal spoon, cutting through the mixture until all the egg white is evenly incorporated.
7. Pour half the mixture into a buttered 1.5 litre/2½ pint soufflé dish. Drain the poached eggs and blot with paper towels.
8. Place the eggs in the soufflé dish and cover with the remaining mixture.
9. Put the dish on a baking sheet. Place in a preheated oven and bake for 30-35 minutes until light and fluffy. Serve immediately.

Swiss fondue

Preparation time: 20-25 minutes
Cooking time: 15 minutes

1 garlic clove, peeled

450 ml/¾ pint dry white wine

1 teaspoon lemon juice

350 g/12 oz Gruyère cheese,
    finely grated

350 g/12 oz Emmenthal cheese,
    finely grated

1 tablespoon cornflour

3 tablespoons Kirsch

salt

freshly ground black pepper

French bread, cut into chunks

1. Cut the garlic clove in half and rub the cut surfaces around a fondue pot or heavy saucepan. Add the wine and lemon juice to the pot and heat gently until just bubbling.
2. Add a little cheese and stir until just melted. Add the remaining cheese, a little at a time, stirring with each addition, until melted.
3. Blend the cornflour with the Kirsch. Stir into the pan and cook over a low heat for about 3 minutes until thickened.
4. Add salt and pepper to taste. Serve immediately. Spear French bread on to long fondue forks and dip into the fondue.

Mayonnaise

Makes about 300 ml/½ pint
Preparation time: 15-20 minutes

2 egg yolks

½ teaspoon salt

freshly ground black pepper

¼ teaspoon dry mustard

¼ teaspoon caster sugar
   (optional)

1 tablespoon wine vinegar

1 tablespoon lemon juice

300 ml/½ pint olive oil

1. Put the yolks, salt, pepper, mustard, sugar, vinegar and lemon juice into a basin and whisk together well.
2. Gradually beat in the oil, drop by drop. As the mixture thickens the oil can be added in a thin stream until completely blended.
3. Taste and adjust the seasoning.

Bearnaise sauce

Makes about 150 ml/¼ pint
Preparation time: 5 minutes
Cooking time: 10-15 minutes

25 g/1 oz chopped shallot

6 peppercorns

1 tablespoon tarragon vinegar

2 egg yolks

25 g/1 oz softened butter

salt

juice of ½ lemon

2 teaspoons chopped fresh
   tarragon

1 teaspoon chopped fresh
   chervil

1. Put the shallot, peppercorns and vinegar into a saucepan, boil to reduce to half quantity, strain into a heatproof basin and allow to cool.
2. Add the egg yolks and whisk over a saucepan of hot water over a low heat, until pale in colour and thick enough to coat the back of a wooden spoon.
3. Gradually whisk in the butter then remove the basin from the heat.
4. Stir in the salt, lemon juice, tarragon and chervil.
5. Serve with steaks and grilled meat.

Hollandaise sauce

Makes about 300 ml/½ pint
Preparation time: 5 minutes
Cooking time: 10-15 minutes

2 tablespoons wine vinegar

2 tablespoons water

3 egg yolks

100 g/4 oz softened butter, cut
   into pieces

2 tablespoons lemon juice

salt

freshly ground black pepper

This sauce can be kept warm by putting the basin over a saucepan of hot water, but do not use any heat.

1. Boil the vinegar in a saucepan until reduced to half quantity, add the water and pour into a heatproof basin.
2. Add the egg yolks, put the basin over a saucepan of hot water over a low heat, and whisk continuously until thick enough to coat the back of a wooden spoon.
3. Gradually whisk in the butter, and then the lemon juice, salt and pepper.
4. Serve the sauce warm with fish, chicken, asparagus or broccoli.

Cheese, celery & grape salad

Preparation time: 10 minutes

4 sticks celery, finely chopped

100 g/4 oz black grapes, halved and seeded

225 g/8 oz Cheshire cheese, crumbled

Dressing:

100 g/4 oz apple purée

3 tablespoons mayonnaise

salt

freshly ground black pepper

This salad can be made several hours in advance. Cover with cling film and chill until needed.

1. Mix the celery, grapes and cheese in a bowl.
2. Mix together the dressing ingredients until smooth. Add to the salad and stir well.
3. Transfer the salad to a serving dish. Garnish with celery leaves, if liked.

Greek salad

Preparation time: 15 minutes

½ Iceberg lettuce, shredded

1 Spanish onion, peeled and thinly sliced

½ cucumber, thinly sliced

2 tablespoons chopped fresh parsley

1 green pepper, cored, seeded and cut into thin strips

3 small tomatoes, cut into small wedges

175 g/6 oz Feta cheese, cut into small cubes

10 black olives

Dressing:

5 tablespoons olive oil

2 tablespoons wine vinegar

1 tablespoon capers, finely chopped

salt

freshly ground black pepper

1. Place the lettuce, onion, cucumber, parsley and green pepper in a salad bowl. Add the tomato wedges to the bowl; mix well.
2. Place all the dressing ingredients in a screw-topped jar. Shake well to mix.
3. Toss the salad in the dressing just before serving. Sprinkle over the cheese and olives.

Green salad with blue cheese dressing

Preparation time: 10 minutes

1 crisp lettuce

Selection of salad leaves, e.g.
  endive, corn salad, spinach

½ cucumber, cut into
  matchstick pieces

1 punnet mustard and cress,
  washed

1 small green pepper, cored,
  seeded and cut into thin strips

1 avocado, halved, skinned and
  thinly sliced

25 g/1 oz walnuts, chopped

Dressing:

100 g/4 oz Stilton or Danish blue
  cheese, grated

150 ml/¼ pint soured cream

1 teaspoon clear honey

salt

freshly ground black pepper

1. Wash the lettuce and salad leaves, and pat dry with paper towels.
2. Shred the leaves with the fingers into a salad bowl. Sprinkle over the cucumber, mustard and cress and green pepper.
3. Arrange the avocado slices in the salad bowl and sprinkle with the walnuts.
4. Mix together the dressing ingredients in a bowl. Pour over the salad and toss just before serving, or serve separately if preferred.

Herbed tomato & Mozzarella salad

Preparation time: 5 minutes

450 g/1 lb tomatoes, thinly sliced

1 Italian Mozzarella (about
  175 g/6 oz), thinly sliced

Dressing:

1 garlic clove, peeled and
  crushed

3 tablespoons olive oil

1 tablespoon lemon juice

salt

freshly ground black pepper

1 tablespoon chopped fresh
  mixed herbs, e.g. oregano, basil,
  parsley, thyme

1. Arrange the tomato slices and cheese in alternate rows on a flat serving plate.
2. Place all the dressing ingredients in a screw-topped jar. Shake well to mix.
3. Pour the dressing over the salad just before serving.

Blue cheese salad

Preparation time: 15 minutes

4 tablespoons oil

1 garlic clove, peeled and crushed

3 thick slices bread, cut into cubes

1 crisp lettuce, shredded

bunch of watercress, trimmed and washed

1 chicory, sliced

225 g/8 oz blue cheese, e.g. Danish blue, Stilton or Roquefort, crumbled or cubed

Dressing:

150 ml/¼ pint plain unsweetened yogurt

2 teaspoons light Dijon mustard

1 teaspoon clear honey

salt

freshly ground black pepper

1. Heat the oil in a frying pan and gently fry the garlic for 1 minute.
2. Add the bread cubes and fry until evenly browned, turning occasionally. Drain the bread cubes on paper towels.
3. Place the lettuce, watercress and chicory in a salad bowl. Toss lightly.
4. Sprinkle the cheese into the bowl with the bread cubes.
5. Mix together the dressing ingredients in a small bowl. Pour over the salad and toss just before serving, or serve separately.

Slimmers' salad

Serves 2 as a main meal
Preparation time: 15 minutes

2 rashers streaky bacon, rinds removed

1 small bunch radishes, trimmed and thinly sliced

1 green pepper, cored, seeded and chopped

½ cucumber, chopped

225 g/8 oz cottage cheese

1 small bunch chives

½ teaspoon finely grated lemon rind

2 tablespoons lemon juice

salt

freshly ground black pepper

1. Grill the bacon until crisp. Drain well on paper towels. Crumble into small pieces.
2. Place the radishes in a bowl with the pepper, cucumber and cheese. Snip the chives into the bowl. Add the lemon rind and juice, salt and pepper; mix well.
3. Transfer the salad to a serving dish and sprinkle with the bacon pieces.

Eggs provençal

Preparation time: 10-15 minutes
Cooking time: 20-25 minutes
Oven: 190°C, 375°F, Gas Mark 5

4 tablespoons oil

225 g/8 oz onions, peeled and sliced

2 garlic cloves, peeled and crushed

225 g/8 oz courgettes, sliced

½ teaspoon mixed dried herbs

2 tablespoons chopped fresh parsley

1 x 400 g/14 oz can tomatoes

salt

freshly ground black pepper

4 eggs

1. Heat the oil in a pan, add the onions and garlic and fry for 3-4 minutes. Add the courgettes and fry for a further 3-4 minutes.
2. Stir in the herbs, parsley, salt, pepper and tomatoes. Put the mixture into an ovenproof dish.
3. Make 4 hollows and break an egg into each. Cook in a preheated oven for 10-15 minutes or until the eggs are set.

Hidden eggs

Preparation time: 10 minutes
Cooking time: 10-15 minutes
Oven: 180°C, 350°F, Gas Mark 4

65 g/2½ oz butter

1 tablespoon finely chopped onion

100 g/4 oz mushrooms, chopped

1 tablespoon chopped fresh parsley

salt

freshly ground black pepper

½ teaspoon dried basil

4 large tomatoes

4 eggs

4 slices buttered toast

watercress, to garnish

1. Use 15 g/½ oz of the butter to grease a shallow, medium ovenproof dish.
2. Melt 25 g/1 oz of the butter in a frying pan, add the onion and mushrooms and fry until soft. Stir in the parsley, salt, pepper and basil.
3. Cut a slice from the top of each tomato, carefully scoop out the pulp and put the tomato shells into the prepared dish.
4. Put some mushroom mixture into each tomato and break an egg on top.
5. Sprinkle with salt and pepper and dot each with the remaining butter. Replace the slice of tomato and cook in a preheated oven for 8-10 minutes or until the eggs are set.
6. Cut rounds of toast slightly larger than the tomatoes and place one under each tomato.
7. Garnish with watercress and serve as a starter.

Chicory & ham bake

Preparation time: 25 minutes
Cooking time: 45 minutes
Oven: 180°C, 350°F, Gas Mark 4

25 g/1 oz butter

4 heads chicory, trimmed

4 tablespoons water

1 tablespoon lemon juice

salt

freshly ground black pepper

4 slices cooked ham

250 ml/8 fl oz milk

75 g/3 oz Gruyère or Cheddar
cheese, grated

2 eggs, lightly beaten

1. Heat the butter in a large saucepan and coat the chicory in butter. Add the water, lemon juice, salt and pepper.
2. Cover and cook gently for about 15 minutes.
3. Remove the chicory from the pan with a slotted spoon. Wrap a slice of ham round each one. Place in a buttered ovenproof dish.
4. Add the milk, cheese, salt and pepper to the eggs. Pour over the chicory.
5. Place in a preheated oven and bake, uncovered, for 30 minutes until the sauce is set and the top is golden brown.

Variations:
Use celery instead of chicory.
Trim 1 head of celery to even lengths. Cook as for the chicory, reducing the cooking time to 10 minutes. Divide the celery sticks between slices of ham and roll up.
Use garlic sausage instead of cooked ham. You will need 8 slices of garlic sausage, 2 for each chicory head.

Aubergine & cheese pie

Preparation time: 25 minutes
Cooking time: 45 minutes
Oven: 200°C, 400°F, Gas Mark 6

2 medium aubergines

1 egg, beaten

75 g/3 oz wholewheat
   breadcrumbs

6 tablespoons olive oil

1 x 400 g/14 oz can tomatoes

½ teaspoon dried oregano

1 garlic clove, peeled and
   crushed

1 teaspoon sugar

salt

freshly ground black pepper

175 g/6 oz Mozzarella cheese,
   thinly sliced

4 tablespoons grated Parmesan
   cheese

1. Cut the aubergines into 5 mm/¼ inch thick slices. Brush the slices with the beaten egg, then coat in the breadcrumbs.
2. Heat half the olive oil in a large pan and fry half the aubergine slices for about 5 minutes, turning once, until golden brown. Remove from the pan. Heat the remaining oil and fry the remaining aubergine slices.
3. Place the tomatoes, oregano, garlic, sugar, salt and pepper in a liquidizer. Blend until smooth. Alternatively, press through a sieve.
4. Place the aubergines in a 2.25 litre/4 pint ovenproof dish. Sprinkle with salt and pepper. Cover with the Mozzarella cheese, then pour over the tomato sauce.
5. Sprinkle with the Parmesan cheese. Place in a preheated oven and cook, uncovered, for 35 minutes.

Cheese & tomato pudding

Preparation time: 20 minutes, plus
standing
Cooking time: 30-40 minutes
Oven: 200°C, 400°F, Gas Mark 6

4 large slices bread, crusts
   removed

3 eggs, separated

300 ml/½ pint milk

½ teaspoon salt

freshly ground black papper

175 g/6 oz Double Gloucester
   cheese, grated

4 tomatoes, skinned, seeded and
   chopped

2 teaspoons Worcestershire
   sauce

1. Break up the bread and place in a bowl with the egg yolks. Place the egg whites in a separate bowl.
2. Heat the milk to just below boiling. Pour over the bread and mix with a fork. Leave for 20 minutes.
3. Add salt, pepper and the cheese to the bread. Mix well.
4. Whisk the egg whites until stiff. Fold into the cheese mixture, cutting through with a metal spoon, until all the egg white is incorporated.
5. Place the tomatoes in a buttered 1.75 litre/3 pint ovenproof pie dish. Sprinkle with the Worcestershire sauce and cover with the cheese mixture.
6. Place in a preheated oven and bake for 30-40 minutes until risen and golden brown. Serve immediately.

Omelette à la crème

Serves 1
Preparation time: 10 minutes
Cooking time: 3-5 minutes

50 g/2 oz cheese, grated

3 tablespoons single cream

3 eggs

3 teaspoons water

salt

freshly ground black pepper

15 g/½ oz butter

4 asparagus spears

1. Mix together the cheese and cream.

2. In a separate bowl beat together the eggs, water, salt and pepper.

3. Melt the butter in an omelette pan and when sizzling hot pour in the egg mixture.

4. Using a wooden spatula keep the liquid egg moving all the time bringing it from the edge of the pan into the centre.

5. When most of the egg has set spread the omelette out to the sides of the pan and allow it to settle for 1-2 seconds, then fold over one-third of the omelette away from the handle.

6. Place half of the cheese mixture along the centre of the omelette and push the omelette down the pan so that it is just coming out of the sides.

7. Hold the pan from underneath the handle and tip the pan over so that the omelette folds out on to a flameproof serving plate.

8. Arrange the asparagus on top and cover with the remaining cheese mixture.

9. Place under a preheated hot grill for a few seconds until the cheese has melted.

10. Serve as a light meal with a salad, or as a main meal with grilled tomatoes and a baked potato.

Granary cheese plait

Preparation time: 30 minutes, plus rising
Cooking time: 35 minutes
Oven: 220°C, 425°F, Gas Mark 7

250 ml/8 fl oz warm water

2 teaspoons sugar

2 teaspoons dried yeast

450 g/1 lb granary flour

2 teaspoons salt

25 g/1 oz lard

1 medium onion, peeled and grated

225 g/8 oz Cheshire cheese, grated

1. Measure the water into a jug. Sprinkle over the sugar and yeast. Leave for about 10 minutes until frothy.
2. Place the flour and salt in a mixing bowl. Add the lard and rub into the flour with the fingertips.
3. Add the onion, cheese and yeast liquid and mix to form a soft dough.
4. Turn out on to a floured surface and knead for about 5 minutes until smooth and elastic.
5. Place the dough in a large oiled polythene bag and leave to rise for about 1 hour until doubled in size.
6. Knead the dough again for 2 minutes and divide into 3 equal pieces. Shape each into a long sausage shape.
7. Plait the pieces of dough together, pinching the ends to seal. Place the plait on a greased baking sheet and cover with oiled polythene. Leave to prove for about 40 minutes until well risen.
8. Sprinkle the plait lightly with flour. Place in a preheated oven and bake for about 35 minutes until golden brown. To test the bread is cooked, tap the base; it will sound hollow when cooked.
9. Cool on a wire tray and serve warm or cold.

Hot cheese & onion bread

Preparation time: 10 minutes
Cooking time: 20 minutes
Oven: 200°C, 400°F, Gas Mark 6

4 spring onions, finely chopped

75 g/3 oz butter, softened

100 g/4 oz Gruyère cheese, grated

salt

freshly ground black pepper

1 small crusty loaf

1. Place the onions, butter, cheese, salt and pepper in a bowl. Beat with a wooden spoon until well mixed.
2. Make cuts down the loaf at 2.5 cm/1 inch intervals almost to the base.
3. Spread the cheese mixture over each slice of bread.

Leicester scone round

Preparation time: 15 minutes
Cooking time: 25-30 minutes
Oven: 200°C, 400°F, Gas Mark 6

225 g/8 oz self-raising flour

1 teaspoon salt

50 g/2 oz block margarine

175 g/6 oz Leicester cheese, grated

175 g/6 oz cooking apple, peeled, cored and grated

1 egg, beaten

2 tablespoons milk

beaten egg or milk, to glaze

sesame seeds

1. Place the flour and salt in a mixing bowl. Add the margarine, cut into small pieces, and rub into the flour with the fingertips until the mixture resembles fine breadcrumbs.
2. Stir in two-thirds of the cheese and all the apple; mix well.
3. Add the beaten egg and milk and mix to form a soft dough.
4. Turn out on to a floured surface and knead lightly until smooth.
5. Roll out to an oblong, 30 x 23 cm/12 x 9 inches. Sprinkle with the remaining cheese and brush the edges with water.
6. Roll up from one long edge. Place on a greased baking sheet and curl round to form a ring.
7. Make deep cuts around the ring at 2.5 cm/1 inch intervals almost to the base.
8. Brush with beaten egg or milk and sprinkle with sesame seeds. Place in a preheated oven and bake for 25-30 minutes until golden brown. Serve warm.

Peanut cheese biscuits

Makes about 35
Preparation time: 15 minutes
Cooking time: 15 minutes
Oven: 190°C, 375°F, Gas Mark 5

175 g/6 oz plain flour

50 g/2 oz wholemeal flour

½ teaspoon salt

100 g/4 oz butter

1 tablespoon made English mustard

100 g/4 oz Cheddar cheese, grated

75 g/3 oz salted peanuts, finely chopped

1 egg, beaten

2 tablespoons milk

beaten egg, to glaze

1. Place the flours and salt in a mixing bowl. Add the butter, cut into small pieces, and rub into the flour with the fingertips until the mixture resembles fine breadcrumbs.
2. Add the mustard, cheese and nuts; mix well.
3. Add the beaten egg and milk and mix to form a firm dough.
4. Turn out on to a floured surface and knead lightly until smooth.
5. Roll out thinly and cut into 6 cm/2½ inch rounds with a fluted pastry cutter. Gather together the trimmings and cut out more biscuits.
6. Place the biscuits, a little apart, on baking sheets. Brush with beaten egg.
7. Place in a preheated oven and bake for about 15 minutes until golden brown. Cool on a wire tray.

Coffee meringue bombe

Serves 6-8
Preparation time: 20-25 minutes
Cooking time: 45-60 minutes
Oven: 180°C, 350°F, Gas Mark 4

15 g/½ oz butter

25 g/1 oz caster sugar

Meringue:

4 egg whites

50 g/2 oz granulated sugar

1 tablespoon instant coffee powder

175 g/6 oz caster sugar

Topping:

300 ml/½ pint double or whipping cream

1 x 300 g/11 oz can mandarin oranges, well drained, or thin slices of fresh orange

chocolate dessert topping (optional)

1. Use the butter to grease a 1 litre/2 pint basin and coat the inside with the caster sugar. Place the basin in a roasting tin with warm water about 5 cm/2 inches up the basin.

2. Whisk the egg whites until stiff.

3. Mix together the granulated sugar and coffee and gradually whisk into the egg whites.

3. Fold in the caster sugar and pour the mixture into the prepared basin.

4. Cook on a low shelf in a preheated oven, for 45-60 minutes, until well risen above the basin and firm to the touch.

5. Remove the basin from the water and leave for 10 minutes, then turn the basin upside down on to a serving plate. Remove the basin when cool.

6. Whip the cream until thick and use to cover the meringue.

7. Decorate with the oranges and dribble the chocolate sauce over.

Almond cheesecake

Preparation time: 30 minutes
Cooking time: 1 hour, plus cooling
Oven: 200°C, 400°F, Gas Mark 6;
160°C, 325°F, Gas Mark 3

100 g/4 oz plain flour

65 g/2½ oz soft (tub) margarine

25 g/1 oz caster sugar

1 egg yolk

Cheesecake:

225 g/8 oz full fat soft (cream) cheese

225 g/8 oz cottage cheese, sieved

100 g/4 oz softened butter

50 g/2 oz ground almonds

few drops of almond essence

4 tablespoons honey

4 eggs, beaten

50 g/2 oz flaked almonds

1. To make the pastry, place the flour, soft margarine, sugar and egg yolk in a mixing bowl. Mix with a fork to form a firm dough.
2. Turn out on to a floured surface and knead lightly until smooth. Form into a round and press evenly into the base of a greased 20 cm/8 inch loose-bottomed cake tin. Prick the pastry with a fork.
3. Place in a preheated oven and bake for 15 minutes until light golden brown. Remove from the oven.
4. Beat together the cheeses and butter until smooth. Stir in the ground almonds, almond essence and honey.
5. Gradually beat in the eggs until the mixture is smooth. Pour into the cake tin and sprinkle evenly with flaked almonds.
6. Reduce the oven temperature and bake for 45 minutes, then turn off the oven and open the door slightly. Cool the cheesecake in the oven.
7. Serve the cheesecake at room temperature.

Coeur à la crème

Preparation time: 10 minutes plus chilling

225 g/8 oz cottage cheese, sieved

150 ml/¼ pint double cream

150 ml/¼ pint soured cream

1 egg white

50 g/2 oz icing sugar, sifted

few drops of vanilla essence

To serve:

caster sugar, optional

double cream, optional

450 g/1 lb soft summer fruits

1. Mix together the cottage cheese, double cream and soured cream.
2. Whisk the egg white until stiff and dry. Whisk in the icing sugar and vanilla essence.
3. Fold the meringue into the cream mixture, cutting through the mixture until all the meringue is incorporated.
4. Have ready 4 heart-shaped coeur à la crème moulds on a tray, or line a large sieve with muslin and place over a bowl. Place the mixture in the moulds or lined sieve, pressing down well.
5. Place in the refrigerator and leave for about 8 hours until the cream is firm.
6. Turn the moulds or mould out on to a serving dish. Sprinkle with a little sugar and pour over a little cream, if liked. Serve with soft summer fruits.

Apricot cream flan

Serves 6
**Preparation time: 30 minutes, plus
chilling time**
Cooking time: 25 minutes
Oven: 200°C, 400°F, Gas Mark 6

200 g/7 oz plain flour

pinch of salt

1 tablespoon icing sugar

100 g/4 oz butter

1 egg yolk

cold water

Filling:

1 egg

1 egg yolk

50 g/2 oz caster sugar

40 g/1½ oz plain flour

300 ml/½ pint milk

2-3 drops vanilla essence

Topping:

1 x 425 g/15 oz can apricot
   halves, drained, reserving
   2 tablespoons juice

5 tablespoons apricot jam

1 tablespoon Cointreau
   (optional)

25 g/1 oz flaked almonds, toasted

150 ml/¼ pint double or
   whipping cream, whipped, to
   serve

1. Sift the flour, salt and icing sugar into
a basin. Cut the butter into pieces, add
to the flour and rub in, to resemble fine
breadcrumbs.
2. Add the egg yolk and enough cold
water to mix to a firm dough. Knead well,
wrap the dough in foil and chill in the
refrigerator for at least 1 hour.
3. To make the filling, put the whole egg,
yolk and sugar into a basin and beat until
creamy.
4. Blend the flour with a little of the cold
milk and stir into the egg and sugar
mixture. Bring the remaining milk to the
boil and stir into the egg mixture. Return to
the saucepan, and stirring constantly,
simmer for 2-3 minutes. Stir in the essence.
5. Pour the custard into a basin, cover with
a piece of foil or cling film and leave until
cold.
6. Roll out the pastry and use to line a
20 cm/8 inch flan ring placed on a baking
sheet. Bake blind in a preheated oven for
20-25 minutes. When cooked remove the
flan ring and cool the flan case on a wire
tray.
7. Transfer the flan case to a plate, fill with
the custard and arrange the apricots on
top, leaving an edge of custard showing all
round.
8. Heat together the apricot jam, juice and
Cointreau. Bring to the boil and simmer for
2-3 minutes. When cool spoon over the
apricots. Leave to go completely cold.
9. Sprinkle with the almonds. Serve with
the cream in a bowl.

Soufflé omelette Grand Marnier

Serves 2
Preparation time: 10-15 minutes
Cooking time: 6-7 minutes

2 eggs, separated

2 teaspoons water

4 teaspoons caster sugar

15 g/½ oz butter

75 g/3 oz fresh fruit, peeled and
  sliced, or well drained canned
  fruit, e.g. bananas or apricots

2 tablespoons Grand Marnier,
  warmed

1. Beat together the egg yolks, water and half of the sugar until creamy and light in colour.

2. Whisk the whites until stiff and fold into the yolk mixture.

3. Melt the butter in an 18-20 cm/7-8 inch omelette pan, pour in the mixture and cook over a low heat until most of the egg mixture has set and the underneath is light golden brown.

4. Put the omelette pan under a preheated hot grill for 1-2 minutes to set the top of the omelette.

5. Make a slit across the centre of the omelette, place the fruit close to the slit and fold the omelette in half away from the pan's handle.

6. Hold the pan from underneath the handle and tilt the pan over so that the omelette falls out on to a flameproof plate.

7. Sprinkle with the remaining sugar, pour over the Grand Marnier and ignite.

Apple & cheese pie

Preparation time: 25 minutes
Cooking time: 35 minutes
Oven: 200°C, 400°F, Gas Mark 6

275 g/10 oz plain flour

½ teaspoon salt

75 g/3 oz margarine

50 g/2 oz lard

3 tablespoons cold water

Filling:

450 g/1 lb cooking apples, peeled, cored and sliced

½ teaspoon ground cinnamon

100 g/4 oz soft light brown sugar

175 g/6 oz Wensleydale cheese, sliced

50 g/2 oz butter

Glaze:

milk

1. Place the flour and salt in a mixing bowl. Add the margarine and lard, cut into small pieces, and rub into the flour with the fingertips until the mixture resembles fine breadcrumbs. Add the water and mix to form a firm dough.
2. Turn out on to a floured surface and knead lightly until smooth. Wrap in cling film and chill while making the filling.
3. Mix together the apples, cinnamon, brown sugar and cheese.
4. Roll out half the pastry and use to line a 23 cm/9 inch pie plate. Pile half the filling into the pastry case. Cover with cheese slices, then spoon over the remaining filling. Brush the edge of the pastry with milk. Dot the filling with the butter.
5. Roll out the remaining pastry and cover the pie. Press the edges to seal. Trim the edge of the pie with a knife.
6. Gather together the pastry trimmings; roll out thinly and cut into apple shapes. Brush the pie with milk and decorate with the apple shapes, studding each with a clove to resemble a core.
7. Brush the apple shapes with milk to glaze. Sprinkle the pie with sugar. Place in a preheated oven and bake for 35 minutes until the pastry is golden brown. Serve warm with cream.

Sweet cheese with strawberry purée

Serves 6
Preparation time: 10 minutes, plus chilling

225 g/8 oz ripe strawberries (fresh or frozen), hulled and chopped

50 g/2 oz caster sugar

juice of ½ orange

450 g/1 lb medium fat soft (curd) cheese mixed with

6 tablespoons milk or

450 g/1 lb fromage blanc

mint leaves, to decorate

Fromage blanc can be bought in some large supermarkets and delicatessens. It varies in texture, so if you buy a soft-textured one, serve the dessert in bowls rather than on plates.

1. Press the strawberries through a sieve into a bowl, or liquidize and sieve them.
2. Stir in half the sugar and all the orange juice, then chill.
3. Mix the curd cheese or fromage blanc and remaining sugar together. Divide into 6, shape each into a dome and place on serving plates.
4. Drizzle over the strawberry purée just before serving. Decorate with mint leaves.

Cranberry pancakes

Preparation time: 10 minutes
Cooking time: 15 minutes

100 g/4 oz plain flour

pinch of salt

2 eggs

300 ml/½ pint milk

butter for frying

1 x 375 g/13 oz jar whole
  cranberry sauce

Topping:

150 ml/¼ pint soured cream

2 tablespoons demerara sugar

25 g/1 oz flaked almonds, toasted

½ teaspoon ground cinnamon

2 tablespoons sherry

1. Sift together the flour and salt into a basin. Add the eggs and gradually beat in the milk.

2. In a 13-15 cm/5-6 inch pan, melt a little butter and use the batter to make 8-12 pancakes.

3. Divide the cranberry sauce between the pancakes, roll up and put into a shallow flameproof dish. Keep warm.

4. To make the topping, mix together the soured cream, half of the sugar, almonds, cinnamon and sherry. Pour over the pancakes and sprinkle on the remaining sugar.

5. Put the dish under a preheated grill for several minutes until the sugar has melted and the top is a golden brown.

Notes

1. All recipes serve four unless otherwise stated.
2. All spoon measurements are level.
3. All eggs are sizes 3, 4, 5 (standard) unless otherwise stated.
4. Preparation times given are an average calculated during recipe testing.
5. Metric and imperial measurements have been calculated separately. Use one set of measurements only as they are not exact equivalents.
6. Cooking times may vary slightly depending on the individual oven. Dishes should be placed in the centre of the oven unless otherwise specified.
7. Always preheat the oven or grill to the specified temperature.
8. Spoon measures can be bought in both imperial and metric sizes to give accurate measurement of small quantities.

Acknowledgements

Photography: Robert Golden and Paul Williams
Photographic styling: Antonia Gaunt
Preparation of food for photography: Mary Cadogan and Heather Lambert
The publishers would like to thank the following companies for their help in the preparation of this book: Divertimenti, Marylebone Lane, London W1; Conran Shop, Fulham Road, London SW3; Sloane Square Tiles, Symons Street, Sloane Square, London SW1.

This edition published 1986 by
Octopus Books Limited
59 Grosvenor Street
London W1
© 1981 Hennerwood Publications Limited

ISBN 0 7064 2585 5

Produced by Mandarin Publishers Limited
Printed in Hong Kong

UNIVERSITY OF WISCONSIN STUDIES
IN LANGUAGE AND LITERATURE
NUMBER 13

MODERN THOUGHT IN THE GERMAN LYRIC POETS FROM GOETHE TO DEHMEL

BY

FRIEDRICH BRUNS

ASSISTANT PROFESSOR OF GERMAN

MADISON
1921

To My Wife

LYDIA DALLWIG BRUNS

"Wem sonst als Dir."

CONTENTS

FOREWORD

The following study seeks to trace the development of a modern view of life as it found expression in the German lyric poets from Goethe to Dehmel. I have limited the discussion in the main to three closely interrelated problems: the conception of the deity, the question of the freedom of the will, and the valuation of life. That I begin with Goethe needs no apology. Adapting the famous word of Matthew Arnold, we can say: As he is our greatest, he is also our first modern man. Even Schiller belongs to a former age. Goethe, as Wilhelm Dilthey puts it, was the first poet to understand and interpret life in terms of itself, free from any traditional view or dogma.

Although this study is chiefly concerned with lyric poetry, I have not rigidly excluded other sources: diaries, letters, and prose works. It was necessary to draw upon these more fully in the case of Novalis and Nietzsche. The small body of finished poetical production of Novalis does not yield a complete picture of his *Weltanschauung;* a closer study of his *Fragmente* and diaries is indispensable to this end and throws new light on his lyrics. Nietzsche also deserves to rank with the great lyric poets, although the body of his verse is small. In his case, too, it was necessary to draw more fully on his other works, especially *Also sprach Zarathustra.* This work, a philosophical epic in rhythmic prose, is clearly the product of a great lyric genius, and is in great part purely lyric in character. Furthermore, a study of Nietzsche is indispensable to a full understanding of German literature since 1890. The chapter on Nietzsche is the necessary introduction to my study of Dehmel. An absolute limitation to lyric verse for the sake of mere consistency seemed neither feasible nor desirable.

The introductory chapter, in which the development of the aforementioned problems in German philosophy is traced, rests largely on secondary sources. I am indebted above all to M. Kronenberg's *Geschichte des deutschen Idealismus*[1] and Kuno Fischer's *Geschichte der neueren Philosophie.*[1] I have also made use of Richard Falckenberg's *Geschichte der neueren Philosophie,*

Oswald Külpe's *Einleitung in die Philosophie*, Friedrich Paulsen's *Einleitung in die Philosophie*[1] and his *Kant*, Ernst Bergmann's *Fichte als Erzieher zum Deutschtum*,[1] Wilhelm Dilthey's
Leben Schleiermachers[1] and the introduction of Fritz Medicus
to his fine new edition of Fichte.   For rapid orientation Rudolph
Eisler's *Philosophisches Wörterbuch*[1] furnished valuable aid.
The sole purpose of this chapter is to supply the necessary
general background for the following study.

I am indebted to my friends and colleagues for criticism and
suggestion, especially to Professor M. C. Otto and Professor
A. R. Hohlfeld.   The former discussed at length with me the
introductory chapter; the latter's fine scholarship, exact and
yet tolerant of other views, was especially helpful in the chapter
on Goethe.   Such friendly help is a boon indeed.

---

[1] Quoted as Kronenberg, Fischer, Paulsen, Bergmann, Dilthey, Eisler.

INTRODUCTION

The fundamental concepts that shaped the view of life in Germany during the eighteenth century were theism, optimism, and free will. This is in marked contrast to France and England, where deism and determinism had gained a far more general acceptance.[1] While Leibniz, *der Vater der Aufklärung*, was the predominant influence in Germany, the deterministic tendency of his system was gradually eliminated. This system itself, in its conciliatory nature, had left an opening for freedom of the will. Our will is motivated, but only by inner impulses that remain partly subconscious; these motives, furthermore, do not exert an absolutely compelling force ("incliner, sans necessiter").[2] Leibniz's theory of the monads made possible individual free will and introduced into his mechanistic conception of the Universe a certain organic trend, since each monad, as each individual, is swayed by inherent inner forces. This seems the initial step to an organic view of the Universe and of life. Thus a few decades later the mechanistic pantheism of Spinoza changed into a vitalistic pantheism in Goethe.[3] Leibniz, however, feared to connect his metaphysics with the "atheist" Spinoza. As he thus avoided pantheism, so his conciliatory nature prevented him likewise from carrying his essentially deistic system of thought to its logical conclusion, and he allowed theism to stand. As Kuno Fischer puts it: "Leibnizens grosser Verstand wollte lieber mehr orthodox scheinen, als weniger folgerichtig denken. Er stellte den reinen Deismus neben die geoffenbarte Theologie, beiden Systemen ihre Eigenart unverletzt verwahrend, und überliess es der Zukunft, einen Gegensatz zu entdecken und auszubilden, wofür sein Zeitalter noch nicht gemacht war."[4]

The most popular work of Leibniz was the *Théodicée,* and its complete title is a sort of confession of faith for the whole period: *Essais de théodicée sur la bonté de Dieu, la liberté de*

[1] Dilthey. 79-83.
[2] Eisler. 2, 769.
[3] Gundolf. 270.
[4] Fischer. 3, 576.

l'homme et l'origine du mal. Evil itself was but a means to make the best of all worlds possible.[5] A popularized Leibniz—this was Wolff's work—ruled in the world of thought till Kant came. Although Kant broke the fetters of dogmatic rationalism, he left the prevalent theistic view of the world untouched, even though, as Friedrich Paulsen says, a pantheistic conception is perceptible beneath the surface.[6] The beginning of a new epoch is brought about by the revival of Spinoza. For over a century the Ethics—to quote Friedrich Paulsen—had been considered the most nefarious of all books and its author a man with the mark of Cain on his brow.[7] While the philosophers still spoke of Spinoza "as of a dead dog", Lessing tells Jacobi that his faith is that of Spinoza: "Die orthodoxen Gottesbegriffe sind nicht mehr für mich, ich kann sie nicht geniessen. Εν και πᾶν! Ich weiss nichts anderes!"[8] With the theistic conception Lessing rejects the belief in freedom of the will; he tells Jacobi: "Ich merke, Sie hätten gerne Ihren Willen frei. Ich begehre keinen freien Willen."[9] The neo-Spinozistic movement first gains fuller expression in Herder. Goethe marks a further step in this development. In a letter to F. H. Jacobi (June 9, 1785) he called Spinoza, because God and existence are identical to him, "theissimum, ja christianissimum."[10] Similarly, before the eighteenth century closed, Novalis called the "atheist" Spinoza "einen gott-trunkenen Menschen,"[11] and Schleiermacher, the greatest theologian since the Reformation, celebrated him in his *Reden über die Religion* as the religious philosopher who was a seeker after God.[12] From that time on, pantheism in one form or other has been the most prevalent view. The belief in an extra-mundane creator eliminated, the mechanistic conception of the Universe was doomed. While even Leibniz had defined organisms as "natural machines," which in their smallest parts are again machines,[13] Schelling

---

[5] Fischer. 3, 586.
[6] Paulsen. 325.
[7] Paulsen. 318.
[8] Jacobi, F. H. *Werke.* (1812-25) 4, 54.
[9] *Ibid.* 4, 61.
[10] W. A. IV, 7, 62.
[11] Novalis. 2, 292.
[12] Schleiermacher. *Reden über die Religion* (Hendel). 47.
[13] Eisler. 2, 62.

declares that the fundamental character of organization is its absolute removal from mechanism[14] and defines the Universe as an "Allorganismus."[15]   To the poets the mechanistic conception of the Universe seems to have given but little inspiration. Schiller's *Lied an die Freude* offers the only real example of which I am cognizant in his famous metaphor of "die grosse Weltenuhr."   The stanza, by the way, stands in marked contrast to the rest of the poem, all the other metaphors being vitalistic.   A poet cannot look upon nature as a machine; he needs must conceive nature as animated, filled with the same life that glows in him.   Thus a poet is predestined to an organic view of life and to pantheism.   A similar trend is apparent in the mystics of all ages.

This pantheism leans towards humanism from the very beginning.   Fichte, in whom the Neo-Platonic idealism of Kant first began to merge with the Neo-Spinozistic current, reaches the conclusion that God lives solely in the human will and consciousness.   Hegel and his school teach that only in the human spirit does the theistic principle attain to consciousness and really become God.   Schelling, following close upon Fichte, says that free creative action is the true nature of man and calls the traditional belief in God immoral.   While Fichte's pantheism is ethical and Hegel's logical, Schelling's is naturalistic.   Only one more step is necessary and we have the absolute humanism of Feuerbach and Nietzsche.   The theistic principle seems entirely eliminated; it reasserts itself in the more mystic Richard Dehmel.

It must be clear from the foregoing how closely this new pantheism is bound up with the problem of the freedom of the will.   The monadic theory of Leibniz led to an accentuation of individualism and the individual.   The revival of Spinoza weakened on the one hand the belief in individual endeavor, and on the other hand, in its new vitalistic aspect, stimulated creative idealism.   Thus a difference of viewpoint between the eighteenth and the nineteenth century develops, which is clearly evident in their respective conceptions of the state. To the eighteenth century the state is chiefly a repressive

---

[14] Eisler.   2, 62.
[15] *Ibid*.   2, 859.

mechanism, and the ideal state is the one that interferes least with the individual. The state is not an organic entity, but a mechanism imposed upon a loose aggregation of individuals. Thus it is small wonder that the century tended towards cosmopolitanism—Dr. Johnson's famous definition of patriotism is equalled by Lessing's statement that patriotism was a virtue he gladly did without—the doctrine of eternal peace is in good part an outcome of this tendency. To the nineteenth century the state is a living organism; the century is intensely nationalistic, and war becomes but an aspect of the struggle for existence that pervades all life. This intense nationalism foredoomed to failure in our day the idea that all mankind is one organism. On this idea the hope of a new internationalism rests. The state, however, conceived as an organic entity, imposes far greater restrictions on the individual; it must even seek to direct the creative energy of each citizen.

The idealism of liberty, which marked the eighteenth century, found full expression in Kant and Schiller. Kant postulated the freedom of the will as an ethical necessity, and Schiller became his most ardent disciple. In his first dramas and his last drama alike Schiller celebrates the hero that seeks to throw off the fetters of tyranny. Only in his *Wallenstein* and *Die Braut von Messina,* under the influence of current romantic tendencies and the study of ancient Greek tragedy, does an all-controlling destiny play an important part. In his lyrics the poet's cherished conviction is summed up in the words:

> Der Mensch ist frei geschaffen, ist frei
> Und würd' er in Ketten geboren.
> (*Die Worte des Glaubens*)

Only a month before his death, in a letter to Wilhelm von Humboldt, Schiller affirms his faith that man is the master of all things: "Am Ende sind wir doch beide Idealisten and würden uns schämen, uns nachsagen zu lassen, dass die Dinge uns formten und nicht wir die Dinge."[16] Schiller's conception of freedom is deeply ethical and excludes arbitrary wilfullness: freedom is achieved only by making the universal world-will

[16] Schiller. *Briefe.* Apr. 2, 1805. (Ed. Jonas). 7, 226.

one's own.   This idea is best expressed in *Das Ideal und das Leben:*

> Nehmt die Gottheit auf in euren Willen
> Und sie steigt von ihrem Weltenthron.
> Des Gesetzes strenge Fessel bindet
> Nur den Sklavensinn, der es verschmäht;
> Mit des Menschen Widerstand verschwindet
> Auch des Gottes Majestät.

Similarly Kant limits individual freedom.   In his *Träume eines Geistersehers* he finds that a secret power within us forces us to have regard for the woe and welfare of others even against our own selfish inclinations.   Thus we are dependent in our innermost motives on the law of a universal will, which is an aspect of a moral unity in the spiritual world, compared by Kant to Newton's law of gravitation in the material world. As a material being man is but a link in the causal chain, but as an "intelligibler Charakter" man is free and this "intelligibler Charakter" is the unmistakable mysterious root of the "empirische Charakter."   Thus Kant, like Schiller, places the main emphasis on the freedom of the will.   The Romanticists in their chief spokesman Friedrich Schlegel were wont to proclaim Fichte as the supreme prophet of the ego, thus missing the truer and deeper import of Fichte's mission as in our own time many missed the real significance of Nietzsche.   Under the influence of Spinoza Fichte had begun as a determinist. When he became a disciple of Kant he espoused the gospel of freedom and soon was its supreme prophet and most eloquent spokesman: he proclaimed the nobility, the divine nature of man.   The revival of Spinoza, however, had made its indelible imprint on Fichte's philosophy; he looked upon the human world as a moral organism and recommended the study of Spinoza as the best aid to the study of the *Wissenschaftslehre.* As Fichte limits the ego by superimposing an "Überich," he limits the individual by his theory of the state.   How much more Fichte, although he is the supreme prophet of the new gospel of freedom, limits individual endeavor than Kant is especially evident if one compares his idea of the state with the Kantian.   Kant is a cosmopolitan liberal; his conception of the state is individualistic.   Fichte's conception of the state is

centripetal.   There burns in him the flame of an intense nationalism and since the state to him is a living organism his philosophy of the state assumes a strongly socialistic aspect.[17]

The conception of mankind as a moral organism soon became
all prevalent.   It is the basic concept underlying Schelling's
philosophy.   His solution of the conflict between individual
freedom and cosmic necessity approaches Hebbel's (who
places more emphasis on the limitation of the individual) and is
practically the same as Dehmel's.   Schelling's highest ethical
law reads: "Handle so, dass dein Wille absoluter Wille sei, dass
die ganze moralische Welt deine Handlung wollen könne, dass
durch deine Handlung kein vernünftiges Wesen als blosses
Objekt, sondern als mithandelndes Subjekt gesetzt werde."[18]

This limitation of individual will assumes a biological
aspect in Schopenhauer's metaphysics.   Schopenhauer trans-
fers the center of volition from the individual to the race.
Nowhere is this more clear than in his chapter, *Die Meta-
physik der Geschlechtsliebe*, where he teaches that sexual
love is not an expression of the individual; the individual is but
the tool of the world-will.   Thus the individual becomes an
impotent nothing in the flux of things.   Under the direct influence of Schopenhauer the poets of pessimism (Grisebach,
Lorm, etc.) deny absolutely the freedom of the will, denounce
it as a mere phantom.   Kindred notes one can find a generation
earlier in the poets of the *Weltschmerz*.   A counter current
against this complete negation of the individual and of individual endeavor finds expression in Nietzsche and Dehmel.
Again we hear notes that remind us of the proud self-determination of Schiller and of Fichte, but the idea that all individual
endeavor must bow to the world-will has gained more and
more emphasis.   This is due in no small measure to Arthur
Schopenhauer, who has thus exerted a positive influence.
To this must be added another factor: the theory of evolution,
more fully developed in its scientific aspect by Darwin, had
penetrated all spheres of thought, nowhere more than in
Germany, where the fundamental ideas of organic development
had been current since the days of Herder and Goethe.   Thus

---

[17] Kronenberg.   2, 262-65.
[18] *Neue Deduktion des Naturrechts* (1795).   Quoted by Fischer.   7, 295.

the way was opened to a creative idealism on an evolutionary basis. Nietzsche, Dehmel, and Arthur Bonus are the most significant figures in this movement.

The problem of the valuation of life, of optimism or pessimism, *Lebensbejahung* or *Lebensverneinung* to use the more exact German terms, is closely interrelated with the preceding. Nowhere is the contrast between the eighteenth and nineteenth century more marked than in their respective attitudes toward the valuation of life and of suffering. Under the spell of the Leibnizian doctrine of the best of all worlds the eighteenth century conceived it to be man's duty to be happy. Thus the consumptive Hölty in the very clutches of death writes his *Aufmunterung zur Freude* (1776):

> O wunderschön ist Gottes Erde
> Und wert darauf vergnügt zu sein;
> Drum will ich, bis ich Asche werde,
> Mich dieser schönen Erde freun.

In the same year he writes his *Lebenspflichten:*

> Rosen auf den Weg gestreut,
> Und des Harms vergessen.

Life is short, but let us remember that God gave it to us not to grieve in, but to be happy in. The pious B. H. Brockes and the Anacreontic poets all re-echo this praise of the joy of life. Schiller in 1785 in his *Lied an die Freude* celebrates joy as the propelling power in the world-mechanism:

> Freude heisst die starke Feder
> In der ewigen Natur.
> Freude, Freude treibt die Räder
> In der grossen Weltenuhr.

In the nineteenth century we have instead the song of suffering, *Das Lied vom Leide.* In Germany it is the century of the rebirth of tragedy; not only did Kleist, Grillparzer, Hebbel, Richard Wagner, and Hauptmann create the modern tragic drama, but the great tragic poets of the past became vital factors once more, above all Sophocles and Shakespeare.

At this point it is interesting to compare Goethe and Schiller. In *Werther* and *Faust* Goethe conceives tragic suffering as inherent in the very nature of things; even Götz goes down in despair seeing that his ideal of liberty cannot be realized upon earth. The young Schiller, as a social reformer in his earlier dramas, attacks evils made by man and which man ultimately can and will brush aside. This is clearly the case in *Die Räuber*, *Fiesco*, *Kabale und Liebe*, and *Don Carlos*. The same thought recurs in *Tell*.

No philosopher probably has done more to open the eyes of mankind to the tragic suffering of life than Arthur Schopenhauer. In the spiritual world coming events do not only throw their shadows before them, often even a whole current of thought finds embodiment in one personality before the hour has come. When the poets of *Weltschmerz* had hardly uttered their first notes, when the very conditions that led to this movement were just beginning to make themselves felt, Schopenhauer published his chief work, *Die Welt als Wille und Vorstellung* (1818). Even those that would rebel at his metaphysical deductions must bow to his relentless power of observation that seizes upon and bares the very essence of things. What is life? A devouring and a being devoured in every aspect, physical as well as spiritual. And of what does life consist? Of pain and sated monotony. The question, Is life worth while? Schopenhauer answers with an emphatic No. How can it be? It is nothing but a continuous fight with death, a fight that we are foredoomed to lose. In its essence life is senseless suffering. The contention of the so-called optimist that in life joy out-weighs pain, Schopenhauer has made impossible, it would seem, in a classic symbol.   In his *Parerga und Paralipomena* he writes: "Wer die Behauptung, dass, in der Welt, der Genuss den Schmerz überwiegt, oder wenigstens sie einander die Wage halten, in der Kürze prüfen will, vergleiche die Empfindung des Tieres, welches ein anderes frisst, mit der dieses andern."[19] The will that controls this world is blind and aimless. Thus pantheism becomes pansatanism.   In this expressive word O. Liebmann has summed up the fundamental aspects of Schopenhauer's pessimistic system. Or to quote Schopenhauer once more: "Die Welt ist die Hölle, und die Menschen sind einerseits die gequälten Seelen und anderseits die Teufel

[19] Schopenhauer, *Werke*. (Ed. Grisebach). 5, 304.

darin."[20]   The fact that so often the tormentor considers
himself a righteous angel of light adds but a touch of grimness
to this infernal spectacle.

This unrelieved pessimism found artistic expression twice
during the century: first under the influence of the disillusion-
ment that followed the Wars for Liberation in the poets of the
Weltschmerz and in an intensified form in the poets of pessimism
that later came under the spell of Schopenhauer.   The problem
of the nineteenth century was how to achieve an absolute
affirmation of life in the face of this deepened insight into the
tragic suffering of existence.   The only possible way is best
summed up by Max Maurenbrecher in his book *Das Leid:*
"Das Leiden *wollen*, das Tragische gut heissen um der Wirkung
willen, die daraus entsteht: das erst ist die wahre Überwindung
des Pessimismus."   Hölderlin, Hebbel, Nietzsche, and Dehmel
mark the phases in the development to this new optimism,
which is best described by the German term *Lebensbejahung*.

---

[20] Schopenhauer.   5, 313.

GOETHE

The first representative of the modern view of life who broke completely with the traditional views of the eighteenth century was Goethe; in his works the Neo-Spinozistic movement found its first poetic embodiment. Goethe's acquaintance with Spinoza began in the year 1774—Friedrich Jacobi was the intermediary—and in spite of the repugnant outer garb the poet recognized in the forgotten philosopher a kindred spirit. "Geist und Herz, Verstand und Sinn"—Goethe himself tells us in *Dichtung und Wahrheit*—"suchten sich mit notwendiger Wahlverwandtschaft, und durch diese kam die Vereinigung der verschiedensten Wesen zu Stande." What attracted Goethe most in Spinoza was the latter's utter unselfishness, "die grenzenlose Uneigennützigkeit, die aus jedem Satze hervorleuchtet."[21] Thus Goethe paraphrases Spinoza's calm objectivity, his ability to leave out of play entirely his own personality in contemplating the phenomena of nature. This is unselfishness of the highest order and a quality deeply embedded in the poet who ever strove to train his senses to relentless accuracy and who prized so highly his "Fähigkeit, das Auge ganz Licht sein zu lassen."[22] Throughout his long life Goethe looked up to Spinoza in gratitude; in the year 1811, when Jacobi's book *Von den göttlichen Dingen und ihrer Offenbarung* displeased him with its thesis that God hides himself in Nature, he sought refuge in Spinoza's *Ethics*, "mein altes Asyl,"[23] and in a stanza, written probably in 1814, he celebrates Spinoza as "Der Philosoph, dem ich zumeist vertraue." He found in him a confirmation of his own views. As early as 1772 Goethe had denied the doctrine of freedom of the will, saying that freedom was merely a relative, even a negative conception: "denn ohne Bestimmung folglich ohne Zwang, ist nichts möglich, nichts gedenkbar. Freiheit drückt Abwesenheit von einer gewissen Bestimmung aus. Nun, von was für einer? Von einer wesentlichen, innern?

---

[21] J. A.   24, 216.
[22] *Ibid.*   26, 154.
[23] *Ibid.*   30, 265.

Unmöglich."[24]   In Goethe's lyric poetry we have a concrete embodiment of his answer to these metaphysical questions in his odes or hymns, the poems in free verse.   Their composition extends over a decade, from 1772 to 1783; it is the formative period of Goethe's career.   For the spring of 1772 we have *Wanderers Sturmlied*, the hymn of genius, rejoicing proudly in his powers, but fighting bitterly against a hostile world.   In the bitter irony of the closing stanza the poet voices his protest against the galling restrictions that fetter him.   A few months later (winter of 1772 to 1773) *Mahomets Gesang* celebrates genius as triumphant victor; the prophet is the mighty river that carries its weaker brethren to the father, the ocean.   This conception of the deity, embodied in the symbol of the ocean as the beginning and end of all life, is as clearly pantheistic as the poet's attitude to Nature in *Ganymed* and in *Werthers Leiden*.   But while *Mahomets Gesang* lauds genius that wanders its predestined path in victorious triumph, *Adler und Taube*, written about the same time, pictures genius overcome by a hostile fate, overcome, but resenting scornfully the ever ready cheap wisdom of being content with life's little pleasures. For the year 1774 we have in *Schwager Kronos* and *Prometheus* Goethe's mightiest poems of revolt.   In the former poem Kronos, pictured with grotesque humor as a coachman, is urged on to reckless speed by his passenger, the poet.   There is a vaunting heroism that courts destruction in its desire for the fullness of life.   In the *Prometheus* ode we have, on the one hand, a gigantic protest against the established order of things and, on the other, a clear recognition of the Greek idea of fate: Prometheus acknowledges almighty time and eternal fate as the highest lords; they rule Zeus as they rule him.   But while Goethe thus depicts the limitations of human endeavor, he also glorifies our finite privilege: in the battle with fate man forges his predestined form, he becomes what he is.   Jacobi's reading this poem to Lessing called forth the latter's confession of his own Spinozistic faith.   Not Zeus, whom Prometheus defies, is the real God, but the mysterious force that moves the world from within.

---

[24] J. A. 36, 65.

None of the poems of Goethe are more the direct expression of his life's experience than these hymns that were composed during the storm and stress of his youth and during the years when mature calm was gradually evolving from these turmoils. In September 1775 Goethe went to Weimar, against the counsels of his father and of many of his friends, who feared the dangers of court life. The poet himself, though no direct misgivings seem to have troubled him, was cognizant of the danger, but was determined not to shun it. He looked upon life as a venture, as a battle between fate and human bravery and foresight, whose outcome does not rest solely in our hands. This idea Goethe embodies in the poem *Seefahrt*, which he wrote (September 11, 1776) partly in retrospect of his first year in Weimar, partly looking ahead into the future with calm determination. Human foresight is battling with fate; God-sent changing winds drive the steersman aside from his chosen path, and he seems to yield to them in his endeavor to outwit them, ever faithful to his purpose: "treu dem Zweck auch auf dem schiefen Wege." Before the approaching storm and its fury the sailsman furls his sails, while wind and waves toss the boat about like a fearfilled ball. But the hero stands at the rudder, firm of heart whatever the outcome:

> Mit dem Schiffe spielen Wind und Wellen,
> Wind und Wellen nicht mit seinem Herzen:
> Herrschend blickt er auf die grimme Tiefe
> Und vertrauet, scheiternd oder landend,
> Seinen Göttern.

Thus the spirit of rebellion is gradually yielding to quiet resignation. The *Harzreise* marks a further step in this direction. "In wunderbarer Verwirrung meiner Gedanken," as the poet writes to Frau von Stein on the morning of his departure (November 29, 1777), he leaves the confusion of Weimar and its court for the solitude of the Harz in winter. There perhaps the Gods will grant him insight into his soul: he places his entire trust in them. "Die Götter wissen allein, was sie wollen und was sie mit uns wollen; ihr Wille geschehe,"[25] he jots down. The same thought recurs in the poem:

---

[25] Dec. 4, 1777. W A. IV, 3, 190.

Ein Gott hat
Jedem seine Bahn
Vorgezeichnet,
Die der Glückliche rasch zum freudigen
Ziele rennt;
Wĕm aber Unglück
Das Herz zusammenzog,
Er sträubt vergebens
Sich gegen die Schranken
Des ehernen Fadens,
Den die doch bittere Schere
Nur einmal löst.

As he thinks of the unfortunate Hypochondriac ("Wem aber Unglück das Herz zusammenzog") whom he sought to console on this journey, there comes to the poet a feeling of reproach against the injustice of fate, even though, as his heart tells him, it is kindly to him, protecting and guiding him even in his mad venture of climbing the Brocken in the snows and mists of winter. This attempt was a challenge to fate, a symbolical question: Am I to reach my life's goal? He reaches the summit and immediately after the descent he writes to Frau von Stein: "Mit mir verfährt Gott, wie mit seinen alten Heiligen und ich weiss nicht, woher mir's kommt. Wenn ich zum Befestigungszeichen bitte, dass möge das Fell trocken sein und die Tenne nass, so ist's so, und umgekehrt auch; und mehr als alles, die übermütterliche Leitung zu meinen Wünschen! Das Ziel meines Verlangens ist erreicht; es hängt an vielen Fäden, und viele Fäden hingen davon: Sie wissen, wie symbolisch mein Dasein ist."[26] Thus there is present in Goethe, who shaped his course with proud consciousness, a tendency to seek guidance from Providence in life's mysterious pathway as a pious mystic might have done. It is but another expression of the principle that guided him in his studies, a principle, which towards the close of his life he put into the often quoted words: "Das schönste Glück des denkenden Menschen ist, das Erforschliche erforscht zu haben, und das Unerforschliche ruhig zu verehren."[27]

The *Harzreise* marks the entrance to a period of clarity and harmony, of which the two last hymns—*Grenzen der Menschheit*

[26] Dec. 10, 1777. W A. IV, 3, 199.
[27] J. A. 39, 100.

(1780) and *Das Göttliche* (1783) are the finished expression.
Placed in Weimar in a circle of daily duties Goethe has learned
to revere the natural limitations of human existence; the spirit
of rebellion has disappeared and out of the very rhythm of the
lines a subtler ear hears a changed attitude to life, a feeling of
being at peace with the Universe:

> Wenn der uralte
> Heilige Vater
> Mit gelassener Hand
> Aus rollenden Wolken
> Segnende Blitze
> Über die Erde sät,
> Küss' ich den letzten
> Saum seines Kleides,
> Kindliche Schauer
> Treu in der Brust.
> Denn mit Göttern
> Soll sich nicht messen
> Irgend ein Mensch.

Even more calm and clear in the acceptance of the laws that
govern our existence is the last of these hymns, *Das Göttliche:*

> Nach ewigen, ehrnen
> Grossen Gesetzen
> Müssen wir alle
> Unsers Daseins
> Kreise vollenden.

In the former poem Goethe places the chief emphasis on the
natural limitations of finite mortality: eternity is ours only as
we live on in the race:

> Ein kleiner Ring
> Begrenzt unser Leben,
> Und viele Geschlechter
> Reihen sich dauernd
> An ihres Daseins
> Unendliche Kette.

The latter poem does not so much stress our natural limitations
as our privilege, our great human birthright: all other creatures,
the very elements and Nature itself, obey blind necessity;
to us alone is given the freedom of choice.

Nur allein der Mensch
Vermag das Unmögliche:
Er unterscheidet,
Wählet und richtet;
Er kann dem Augenblick
Dauer verleihen.

Er allein darf
Den Guten lohnen,
Den Bösen strafen,
Heilen und retten,
Alles Irrende, Schweifende
Nützliche verbinden.

This is the privilege of human freedom, of human endeavor: as the conscious element in the Universe, man can within certain limits shape the stream of life and determine its direction. It is a fact worth noting that, while in the earlier hymns Goethe uses the Gods as symbols to portray genius, what is best and noblest in humanity has become a symbol of the Divine in this last poem.

This deepened insight, whose gradual development we have followed, brought about a clear harmony that found its finest embodiment in the *Römische Elegien*. They are in this respect an expression of Goethe's philosophy of life. In this harmony the problem of human freedom seems to be sunk in oblivion. But soon after his return from Rome (1788) solitude embitters the poet; he again attacks the old question of freedom and under the influence of the French Revolution it assumes a political aspect. His study of Nature and the natural sciences had deepened his insight into and his faith in the wisdom of gradual evolution, and he must needs condemn this sudden political upheaval as an expression of mere arbitrary endeavor:

Alle Freiheitsapostel, sie waren mir immer zuwider,
Willkür suchte doch nur jeder am Ende für sich.
Willst du viele befreien, so wag' es vielen zu dienen.
Wie gefährlich das sei, willst du wissen? Versuch's.

Thus Goethe espouses the political ideal of Frederick the Great: the prince as the first servant of his people. And yet, kings as well as demagogues are subject to error, no matter how good their intentions, they are human even as the rest of mankind.

The people, however, are blind, and only the great leader can give them a goal:

> Könige wollen das Gute, die Demagogen desgleichen,
> Doch irren sie sich: Menschen, ach, sind sie wie wir.
> Nie gelingt es der Menge für sich zu wollen; wir wissen's.
> Doch wer verstehet für uns alle zu wollen—er zeig's.

Goethe's whole theory of life is marked by a predilection for contrasts; his calm objectivity prevents him from becoming a one-sided partisan. He is not a defender of despotism and reminds those of his contemporaries who had nothing but condemnation for the French Revolution that wisdom is silent in the slave while it may find utterance even in a madman if only free:

> "Jene Menschen sind toll," so sagt ihr von heftigen Sprechern,
> Die wir in Frankreich laut hören auf Strassen und Markt.
> Mir auch scheinen sie toll; doch redet ein Toller in Freiheit
> Weise Sprüche, wenn, ach, Weisheit im Sklaven verstummt.

As he condemns despotism he scorns its loathsome counterpart of servile adulation.   This is his advice to his son:

> Willst du, mein Sohn, frei bleiben, so lerne was Rechtes und halte
> Dich genügsam und nie blicke nach oben hinauf.

Here we have that same genuine democracy, that freedom from empty pomp and ostentation, that are characteristic of Goethe's life.   And what is the practical result of these views?   The epigram *Pflicht für jeden* formulates the best answer to this question:

> Immer strebe zum Ganzen und kannst du selber kein Ganzes
> Werden, als dienendes Glied schliess an ein Ganzes dich an.

Every reader of Nietzsche will here be reminded of the doctrine of greater obedience.   Organic development is the highest controlling principle, every individual is but a part of a greater organism and must thus serve a higher aim.   Goethe denounces all arbitrary individual endeavor, all revolutions, since they annul this first law of life.   In so far as it repressed quiet development he condemned the Protestant Reformation as he condemned the French Revolution.

> Franztum dränget in diesen verworrenen Tagen, wie eh'mals
> Luthertum es getan, ruhige Bildung zurück.

This was written in 1796.   It seems to be part of our mortal lot to become ultra-conservative in those years when the maturity of manhood begins to yield to age.   Goethe did not escape this fate.   It is hardly necessary to enumerate here the factors contributing to this ultra-conservative trend: the recently gained deepened insight into the laws of evolution, the indignation at the excesses of the French Revolution, the disappointment and loneliness after his return from Italy.   The above epigram is not Goethe's last word on the work of Luther. Our poet always prized highly the freedom that we owe to it (compare especially the poem *Dem 31. Oktober 1817* and Eckermann's last conversation with Goethe).   But with all this love of liberty the poet voices ever and again his abiding faith in the wisdom of gradual evolution which limits and even makes impossible arbitrary individual endeavor.   The idea recurs in ever varying form, now borrowing its symbols from astrology, now from oriental fatalism:

> Was machst du an der Welt? sie ist schon gemacht,
> Der Herr der Schöpfung hat alles bedacht.
> Dein Los ist gefallen, verfolge die Weise,
> Der Weg ist begonnen, vollende die Reise:
> Denn Sorgen und Kummer verändern es nicht,
> Sie schleudern dich ewig aus gleichem Gewicht.

Individual freedom is controlled in two ways: on the one hand the individual develops according to the inherent laws of organic growth, which neither time nor external force can change; on the other he is a part of a larger organism, the cosmic all, whose development takes precedence over that of the individual.   Critics who stress the individualistic aspect of Goethe's philosophy love to quote Suleika's famous lines:

> Volk und Knecht und Überwinder,
> Sie gestehn zu jeder Zeit,
> Höchstes Glück der Erdenkinder
> Sei nur die Persönlichkeit.

They should not forget Hatem's, i.e., Goethe's answer to Suleika:

> Kann wohl sein, so wird gemeinet,
> Doch ich bin auf andrer Spur.

Here, as in such poems as the deeply mystical *Selige Sehnsucht*
and *Höheres und Höchstes*, Goethe plainly teaches that the
barriers of individual existence must be overcome:

> Bis im Anschaun ew'ger Liebe
> Wir verschweben, wir verschwinden.

Goethe, of course, was far too much of an individualist to deny
utterly the individual. Here too his love of contrasts is apparent. He has frequently presented both sides of this question
of individual freedom and cosmic necessity. I refer to such
poems as *Die Metamorphose der Tiere, Urworte. Orphisch*, and
Eins und Alles with its pendant *Vermächtnis*. The *Urworte*,
written in October 1817, present the fullest discussion of this
question; the initial poem is entitled Δαιμων, *Dämon*. The
individual develops according to the law that ruled his beginning:

> Wie an dem Tag, der dich der Welt verliehen,
> Die Sonne stand zum Grusse der Planeten,
> Bist alsobald und fort und fort gediehen
> Nach dem Gesetz, wonach du angetreten.
> So musst du sein, dir kannst du nicht entfliehen,
> So sagten schon Sibyllen, so Propheten,
> Und keine Zeit und keine Macht zerstückelt
> Geprägte Form, die lebend sich entwickelt.

Still "Τυχη, das Zufällige," the accidental, chance has its
place in this scheme of things. Man is a social being, he acts
as he sees others act, and thus heredity's iron law is modified
by environment:

> Nicht einsam bleibst du, bildest dich gesellig
> Und handelst wohl, so wie ein andrer handelt.

This is, however, but a semblance of freedom, for through this
very means the world-will forces the individual to fulfill its
bidding. As the years ripen Eros appears, and what seems
individual desire is cosmic necessity. Ἀναγκη, *Nötigung* is
the child of Ἐρως, *Liebe*:

> Da ist's denn wieder, wie die Sterne wollten:
> Bedingung und Gesetz, und aller Wille
> Ist nur ein Wollen, weil wir eben sollten,
> Und vor dem Willen schweigt die Willkür stille.
> Das Liebste wird vom Herzen weggescholten,

> Dem harten Muss bequemt sich Will' und Grille.
> So sind wir scheinfrei denn nach manchen Jahren
> Nur enger dran, als wir am Anfang waren.

Only 'Ελπις, *Hoffnung* gives us the fond belief of freedom from these fetters.   Is this an approach to the passive resignation of fatalism?   This is not Goethe's wish.   Even in *Die Metamorphose der Tiere* (begun 1796, completed 1819), where the very subject would emphasize the law of racial organic development, the poet enunciates clearly that "Macht und Schranken, Willkür und Gesetz, Freiheit und Mass," appear in Nature in eternal union.   Man, who of all creatures enjoys the greatest measure of freedom, does not achieve his destiny merely by passive resignation.   This too is necessary, but out of this surrender of the individual to the world-soul there must be born living activity.   Let the world-soul penetrate us so that we may be better able to wrestle with the world-spirit.   This is our heaven-born destiny:

> Im Grenzenlosen sich zu finden,
> Wird gern der Einzelne verschwinden;
> Da löst sich aller Überdruss.
> Statt heissem Wünschen, wildem Wollen,
> Statt läst'gem Fordern, strengem Sollen,
> Sich aufzugeben ist Genuss.
>
> Weltseele, komm uns zu durchdringen!
> Dann mit dem Weltgeist selbst zu ringen
> Wird unsrer Kräfte Hochberuf.
> Teilnehmend führen gute Geister,
> Gelinde leitend, höchste Meister,
> Zu dem, der alles schafft und schuf.

Here we see again how Goethe's conception of individual freedom and its limitation is interlocked with his pantheism. Thus these verses remind one of the often quoted lines:

> Was wär' ein Gott, der nur von aussen stiesse,
> Im Kreis das All am Finger laufen liesse!
> Ihm ziemt's, die Welt im Innern zu bewegen
> Natur in sich, sich in Natur zu hegen,
> So dass, was in ihm lebt und webt und ist,
> Nie seine Kraft, nie seinen Geist vermisst.

Goethean thought, it would seem to me, forms the portal to a religion of to-day, a religion that is born of the cumulative

experience and insight of the race.   At all events, whatever of
freer religious thought has assumed shape in Germany since his
day, from Hölderlin and Schleiermacher to Nietzsche, Dehmel,
and Arthur Bonus, has received, in varying degree, the imprint
of Goethe.   And is there any endeavor or thought to-day that
could not profit from the mature wisdom of this greatest modern
man, of whom Emerson remarked: "The old Eternal Genius
who built the world has confided himself more to this man
than to any other"?   From Goethe the ultra-radical might
learn the wisdom of gradual evolution as opposed to sudden
arbitrary revolution; his steady insistence that life is change,
that life is ceaseless development, might be equally valuable
to the ultra-conservative; and the modern theorist in education,
believing in the omnipotence of environment, might learn from
him the wisdom of the opposite view.

The poems of Goethe that deal with his valuation of life
bear far less the imprint of metaphysical reasoning than those
so far discussed.   They seem to result much rather from a
feeling of life's overwelling fulness and are the direct expression
of purely emotional impulses.   Goethe was above all a man of
this Earth, and rightly has his *Diesseitigkeit* been so often
stressed.   From his earliest youth his endeavor was to achieve
harmony out of this fulness of joy and sorrow, a difficult task
for one whose over-emotional nature tended to excess in either
direction.   As early as 1767 he had admonished his friend
Behrisch:

> Sei gefühllos!
> Ein leichtbewegtes Herz
> Ist ein elend Gut
> Auf der wankenden Erde.
> (*Drei Oden*)

The first of *Wanderers Nachtlieder*, written in 1776, is a passion-
ate prayer for peace: "Was soll all der Schmerz und Lust?"
And late in life Goethe confessed that he could not bear to
compose a tragedy, calling himself a conciliatory nature:
"Ich bin nicht zum tragischen Dichter geboren, da meine
Natur konziliant ist."[28]   There seems, withall, ever present a
feeling that life with all its changing fulness of joy and pain is a

---

[28] Oct. 31, 1831. W. A. IV, 49, 128.

blessing.   That note is clearly discernible in the songs addressed to Lili Schönemann, it wells forth from the restless rhythm of the first poems to Frau von Stein:

RASTLOSE LIEBE

Dem Schnee, dem Regen,
Dem Wind entgegen,
Im Dampf der Klüfte,
Durch Nebeldüfte,
Immer zu!   Immer zu!
Ohne Rast und Ruh'!

Lieber durch Leiden
Möcht' ich mich schlagen,
Als so viel Freuden
Des Lebens ertragen.
Alle das Neigen
Von Herzen zu Herzen,
Ach wie so eigen
Schaffet das Schmerzen!

Wie, soll ich fliehen?
Wälderwärts ziehen?
Alles vergebens!
Krone des Lebens,
Glück ohne Ruh',
Liebe, bist du!

When his friend Auguste von Stolberg asked the young poet— it was during the first weeks of his tempestuous infatuation for Lili—whether he was happy, he answered: "Ja, meine Beste, ich bin's, und wenn ich's nicht bin, so wohnt wenigstens all das tiefe Gefühl von Freud und Leid in mir."[29]   This is the prelude to the verses that Goethe wrote after the death of his sister; he had learned that the gods bless with infinite joy and infinite pain those whom they love:

Alles geben die Götter, die unendlichen,
Ihren Lieblingen ganz;
Alle Freuden, die unendlichen,
Alle Schmerzen, die unendlichen, ganz.

With this conviction Goethe remained faithful to his optimism, not as the spoiled child of fortune—thus it pleased a shallow world to designate Goethe, whose prophetic sadness Carlyle

---

[29] Jan. 30, 1775.   W. A. IV, 2, 231.

compared to that of Dante—but throughout a long life that had more than its full share of human suffering, that had over and over again accepted the bitter wisdom of renunciation. I refer the reader to *Faust*, to *Tasso*, to the *Marienbader Elegie*. In the year 1828 Goethe concludes a poem, which quivers with an undercurrent of pain, with the words,

> Wie es auch sei, das Leben, es ist gut.
>
> (*Der Bräutigam*)

And in *Faust* Lynkeus the watchman, overlooking the world from his high tower ere the dusk of evening falls, is none other than Goethe himself, who from his vantage point of more than fourscore years—the poem was written in May 1831—looks upon life and the world and pronounces his parting benediction ere the night comes:

> Zum Sehen geboren,
> Zum Schauen bestellt,
> Dem Turme geschworen,
> Gefällt mir die Welt.
>
> Ich blick' in die Ferne,
> Ich seh' in der Näh'
> Den Mond und die Sterne,
> Den Wald und das Reh.
>
> So seh' ich in allen
> Die ewige Zier,
> Und wie mir's gefallen,
> Gefall' ich auch mir.
>
> Ihr glücklichen Augen,
> Was je ihr gesehn,
> Es sei, wie es wolle,
> Es war doch so schön.

Thus with parting gesture Goethe affirms all life, himself as well as the world. The keynote of Goethe's whole endeavor, as of these poems, is a joyous belief in this world. The young man declares his willingness to leave the vastnesses of the heavens to the Gods for a firm footing on this Earth:

> Ach, ihr Götter, grosse Götter
> In dem weiten Himmel droben!
> Gäbet ihr uns auf der Erde
> Festen Sinn und frohen Mut:
> O wir liessen euch, ihr Guten,
> Euren weiten Himmel droben.

And the aged poet during his last years praises the world with whimsical humor as a precious salad that was a joy to the senses to feast upon early and late:

> Die Welt ist wie ein Sardellensalat.
> Er schmeckt uns früh, er schmeckt uns spat:
> Zitronenscheibchen rings umher,
> Dann Fischlein, Würstlein und was noch mehr
> In Essig und Öl zusammenrinnt,
> Kapern, so künftige Blumen sind—
> Man schluckt sie zusammen wie ein Gesind.

In conclusion I quote an aphorism from the *Maximen und Reflexionen*, that inexhaustible source of Goethean wisdom: "Das Höchste, was wir von Gott und Natur erhalten haben, ist das Leben, die rotierende Bewegung der Monas um sich selbst, welche weder Rast noch Ruhe kennt."[30]

---

[30] W. A. II, 6, 216.

ROMANTICISM

It is interesting to watch the Neo-Spinozistic movement gradually gaining more and more momentum and finally taking over into itself its counter current, the rebirth of Platonic idealism which begins with Kant. This process begins with Fichte and is completed with Schelling, the philosopher of Romanticism. Fichte had left a deep imprint on the rising generation. It is small wonder that the pantheism of Novalis and Hölderlin is more marked and definite than that of Goethe. Both of these poets—this separates them from Friedrich Schlegel—looked upon Fichte and Spinoza as closely akin. Hölderlin, even before he had heard Fichte lecture at Jena, studied the *Wissenschaftslehre* and used Spinoza as a commentary as Fichte himself had advised.[31] In a letter to Hegel he names as identical Fichte's absolute ego and Spinoza's substance.[32] Novalis, who refers to Fichte again and again in his aphorisms, says that Spinoza's God and Fichte's God are very similar[33] and calls realistic idealism or Spinozism the one true philosophy. "Die wahre Philosophie ist durchaus realistischer Idealism—oder Spinozism. Sie beruht auf höherm Glauben. Glauben ist vom Idealism unabtrennlich."[34] The words "realistischer Idealism" portray clearly the above mentioned amalgamation of the two main currents of philosophic thought. The close of the quotation shows the admixture of another element present in both Hölderlin and Novalis, namely Christian mysticism, which also left its imprint on Schelling.

NOVALIS

Friedrich von Hardenberg, known as Novalis, born 1772, early in life came under Pietistic influences. Studying under Schiller and Reinhold he felt the lure of philosophy and literature, but with characteristic determination he finished his voca-

---

[31] Hölderlin. Br. 187.
[32] *Ibid.* 257.
[33] Novalis. 2, 183.
[34] *Ibid.* 2, 182.

tional studies, chemistry, mathematics, and law, and had entered upon his professional career when the death of his betrothed, Sophie von Kühn (March 19, 1797, born March 21, 1781), an embodiment of Goethe's Mignon, became to him the portal of a *vita nuova:* suffering assumes a new and deeper meaning, religion becomes the great Orient of life, death is the beginning of the absolute. But the joy of living lured him anew from his poignant grief. At Freiberg Novalis studied geology under the famous Werner; the teacher's scientific insight became to the disciple a mystical philosophy of nature that seeks to unravel life's mystery. A world of poetical plans was unfolding before him, a new love was brightening his pathway, when death came, March 28, 1801.

What were the fundamental influences that shaped the views of Novalis? To Spinoza and Fichte one must add Neo-Platonic and Christian (Moravian) mysticism and the study of the natural sciences. Owing to the extravagant hopes that the discoveries of Galvani had aroused, this study leads to mystical fantastic speculation, which, however, is not without a basis of facts. Of typical eighteenth century thought the influence of Leibniz is still quite marked, and now and then one still meets traces of a mechanistic view. The life experience that merged all these currents into one was the ever present grief over the death of Sophie.

It seems at first a well-nigh impossible task to construct anything like a coherent system from the loose mass of Novalis aphorisms and diaries, to which one must turn because of the relatively small amount of finished poetical production. But closer study soon reveals the general lines of thought, and one underlying idea becomes evident: all life is one, is one great organism. The law of organic development controls the Universe as it controls the individual. The idea that man can only become what he is, that recurs like a refrain ever since the days of Herder and Goethe, we also find in Novalis' aphorisms: "Man kann nur werden, insofern man schon ist."[35] The Universe is a living organism, like the individual, and it is gradually assuming form according to the laws of its past.

---

[35] Novalis. 3, 61.

"Die Welt ist ein System notwendiger Voraussetzungen—
eine Vergangenheit, ein ante eigner Art."[36]   Or: "Die Natur
ist lauter Vergangenheit, ehemalige Freiheit; daher durchaus
Boden der Geschichte."[37]   We shall see later how this makes
man the master of Nature.   All is in continual flux.   There is
no divine right of property: "Die Natur ist Feindin ewiger
Besitzungen.   Sie zerstört nach festen Gesetzen alle Zeichen des
Eigentums, vertilgt alle Merkmale der Formation. Allen
Geschlechtern gehört die Erde; jedes hat Anspruch auf alles.
. . . Das Eigentumsrecht erlischt zu gewissen Zeiten."[38]
This eternal flux, be it observed, obeys fixed laws, and Novalis'
conception of the state excludes mere anarchy and chaos.   The
life principle of his ideal state is the king, the man of higher
birth, who stands above the state.   Every citizen is a part of
the state, is an official and only as such does he receive an
income.[39]   The ideal of Novalis is a socialistic democracy,
whose highest authority is vested in a king.   Thus the state is
an organism in which the collective will takes precedence over
the individual will: "Flucht des Gemeingeistes ist der Tod."[40]
     A fuller discussion of Novalis' attitude to the question of
freedom of the will is necessary at this point.   Novalis had not
been a disciple of Fichte in vain.   When Sophie von Kühn
died he determined to follow her by the mere power of his will
and seek a union with her in the world of the absolute.   Will
he defines as "magisches, kräftiges Denkvermögen."[41] Fate that
weighs us down is naught but the sloth of our spirit, and by wid-
ening and developing our activity ("Tätigkeit") we can change
ourselves into fate.[42]   May we not perhaps gain omnipotence,
he asks, and achieve our will completely?   We must become
masters of our body as of our soul.   Our body is our tool to
form and transform the world—"das Werkzeug zur Bildung
und Modifikation der Welt.   Wir müssen also unsern Körper
zum allfähigen Organ ausbilden.   Modifikation des Werkzeugs

[36] Novalis.   3, 26.
[37] *Ibid.*   2, 311.
[38] *Ibid.*   2, 113.
[39] *Ibid.*   2, 150.
[40] *Ibid.*   2, 132.
[41] *Ibid.*   2, 202.
[42] *Ibid.*   2, 198.

ist Modifikation der Welt."[43]   Man, and especially the poet and philosopher, is the transforming element of Nature; his mission is to give Earth its form: "Zur Bildung der Erde sind wir berufen."[44]   All we need to do is to arm our senses with the necessary tools; the beginning has already been made.[45]   What we call the accidental is but the raw material which we are to transform with our spirit: "Alle Zufälle unseres Lebens sind die Materialien, aus denen wir machen können, was wir wollen. Wer viel Geist hat, macht viel aus seinem Leben."[46]   Or compare the still more daring statement: "Die Denkorgane sind die Weltzeugungs-, die Naturgeschlechtsteile."[47]   Nature obeys the laws of man's choosing; man can direct her activity into a certain channel and she follows it: "Wozu sie einmal veranlasst ist, das bringt sie nach Gesetzen der Trägheit immerfort hervor.   Im Geiste ist der Grund der Vergänglichkeit zu suchen. Perpetuum mobile."[48]   Since the laws of Nature are laws of habit,[49] man can form the world by the very laws that govern it: "Ich werde unbeschadet der Welt und ihrer Gesetze, mittelst derselben, sie für mich ordnen, einrichten und bilden können."[50]   Thus the Romantic philosopher reveals the principles that underlie certain aspects of modern applied science.

Of all creatures man alone is truly free, he is the polarizing principle, "die Substanz, die die ganze Natur unendlichfach bricht, i. e., polarisiert.   Die Welt, des Menschen Welt, ist so mannigfach, als er mannigfach ist."[51]   Thus Novalis enlarges the sphere of individual activity and development to the greatest possible extent.   The inevitable result is the old conflict between world will and individual will, between will and arbitrary desire, *Wille und Willkür*.   The world is to be as I want it to be; originally my will shapes it.   What then, if there is a discrepancy between the two?   The error must be sought

---

[43] Novalis.   2, 118.
[44] *Ibid.*   2, 118.
[45] *Ibid.*   2, 133.
[46] *Ibid.*   2, 124.
[47] *Ibid.*   2, 209.
[48] *Ibid.*   3, 53.
[49] *Ibid.*   3, 104.
[50] *Ibid.*   2, 284.
[51] *Ibid.*   2, 209.

in both of the factors or in one of them; either the world is awry ("ausgeartet") or my opposing will is not my true will.[52] The individual soul must seek to cooperate with the world soul and achieve harmony with it; the goal is "Herrschaft der Welt-seele und Mitherrschaft der individuellen Seele."[53] The world will finds expression by means of the individual will, the world is the result of infinite agreement, "das Resultat eines unend-lichen Einverständnisses."[54] For Novalis mankind is one organism with a collective will and he defines the *appetitus rationalis* as synthetic will.[55] Between soul and soul he postulates a curious interplay and thus emphasizes the pluralis-tic aspect of his monism; humanity is a pluralistic unity. "Gemeinschaft, Pluralism ist unser innerstes Wesen, und vielleicht hat jeder Mensch einen eigentümlichen Anteil an dem, was ich denke und tue, und so ich an den Gedanken anderer Menschen."[56]

Novalis' philosophy is of a transcendental character and seeks the absolute. All life is a development into ever higher spheres until the absolute, i. e., God, is reached. In *Die Lehrlinge von Sais* Novalis has embodied his favorite doctrine that man is the moral force in the Universe; his office is to make all Nature moral.[57] Thus, too, the aged Sylvester tells Heinrich von Ofterdingen that all woe and grief and pain will vanish when only one power rules, the power of conscience, when Nature has become moral, "sittlich und züchtig."[58] Grief and suffering, however, had too potent a meaning for Novalis that he should deny them. Grief had given to him a new interpretation of life; to suffer is the proof of our higher destina-tion: "Jeder Schmerz ist eine Erinnerung unsers hohen Ranges."[59] Misfortune proves that we are treading the path to God; through it alone can we become holy. Did not the Saints of old seek misfortune of their own free choice?[60] Grief and

---

[52] Novalis. 2, 283.
[53] *Ibid.* 3, 33.
[54] *Ibid.* 2, 204.
[55] *Ibid.* 3, 377.
[56] *Ibid.* 3, 36.
[57] *Ibid.* 4, 17 f.
[58] *Ibid.* 4, 231.
[59] *Ibid.* 3, 93.
[60] *Ibid.* 2, 102; 297.

religion ever go hand in hand.[61]   Disease itself is a mark of our distinction: man is born to suffer; the more helpless he is, the more he is open to morality and religion.[62]   For this reason man is more progressive and perfectible than any other creature. "Vergänglichkeit und Gebrechlichkeit ist der Charakter der mit Geist verbundenen Natur.   Er zeugt von der Tätigkeit und Universalität, von der erhabenen Personalität des Geistes."[63] Death itself is a mark of our higher destiny; the world of matter is eternal, changeless: we rise to higher possibilities through death.   "Alles ist von selbst ewig.   Die Sterblichkeit und Wandelbarkeit ist ein Vorzug höherer Naturen.   Ewigkeit ist ein Zeichen (sit venia verbis) zeitloser Wesen.   Synthesis von Ewigkeit und Zeitlichkeit."[64]   Thus we are eternal and mortal, finite and infinite, and the very fact that we are finite and mortal makes possible an ever higher development.   Death is only relative, and our life in part must be a link in a greater universal life.   Death is life, death is the romantic, i. e., transforming principle of life: "Durch den Tod wird das Leben verstärkt."[65]   This reminds one of Goethe: "Leben ist ihre [Nature's] schönste Erfindung, und der Tod ihr Kunst- griff recht viel Leben zu haben."[66]   The difference, however, is apparent: Goethe stands firmly footed on this Earth, Novalis is gazing into the absolute; for Goethe life becomes more mani- fold through death, for Novalis it passes into a higher, i. e., transmundane sphere.   Still the Goethe of the *Westöstliche Diwan* would agree with Novalis that death is a means to overcome the limitations of individual existence and to rise to higher planes.   Compare such poems as *Selige Sehnsucht* and *Höheres und Höchstes* with the following statement of Novalis: "Tod ist Verwandlung, Verdrängung des Individualprinzips, das nun eine neue haltbare, fähigere Verbindung sucht."[67] Thus Novalis ever affirms life: "Alles zu beleben, ist der Zweck des Lebens.   Lust ist Leben.   Unlust ist Mittel zur Lust,

[61] Novalis.   2, 101.
[62] *Ibid.*   2, 223.
[63] *Ibid.*   2, 223.
[64] *Ibid.*   2, 223; 3, 296.
[65] *Ibid.*   3, 35.
[66] J. A.   39, 5.
[67] Novalis.   2, 312.

wie Tod Mittel zum Leben."[68]   Like Nietzsche Novalis makes joy eternal: "Unsere ursprüngliche Existenz ist Lust.   Die Zeit entsteht mit der Unlust.   Daher alle Unlust so lang und alle Lust so kurz.   Absolute Lust ist ewig,—ausser aller Zeit."[69] But Nietzsche's *trunkenes Lied* sings of this Earth; Novalis again seeks transmundane spheres.   Thus too when Novalis praises the *Théodicée* of Leibniz as a work in which the pulse of the coming life is stirring, and when he makes the belief in the best of all worlds an ethical demand, he has in mind that same future ideal.[70]

As Novalis makes suffering a relative thing, a means to a higher end, so also sin is but the necessary step to the ultimate goal, the morality of Nature; thus he can say: "Dem echt Religiösen ist nichts Sünde."[71]   Evil too is merely relative; it is possible that man may gradually make himself absolutely evil and thus create an absolute evil, but what is evil and bad is only an artificial product which we should annihilate according to the laws of morality and poetry and not believe or accept.[72] In the final stage all evil will be eliminated, even as there is no evil for God.[73]   In this clarifying evolution nothing perishes, everything lives on in a higher sphere: "Die wirkliche Natur ist nicht die ganze Natur.   Was einmal dagewesen lebt fort, nur nicht in der wirklichen Natur."[74]   The world and God are both still in the process of formation: "Die Welt ist noch nicht fertig, so wenig wie der Weltgeist; aus Einem Gott soll ein Allgott werden, aus Einer Welt ein Weltall."[75]   Until this process is completed God and Nature are two separate entities: God is the final goal with which Nature is to attain harmony; he is the world soul of the ideal world.[76]   Fichtean conceptions play an important part: again and again Novalis emphasizes activity, "Tätigkeit"; all being is activity, and God he defines as "unendliche Tätigkeit."[77]   Man is the revealing medium, and he is

[68] Novalis.   3, 71; 2, 113.
[69] *Ibid.*   2, 12.
[70] *Ibid.*   2, 250; 3, 314.
[71] *Ibid.*   3, 111.
[72] *Ibid.*   2, 280.
[73] *Ibid.*   3, 26.
[74] *Ibid.*   3, 378.
[75] *Ibid.*   2, 220.
[76] *Ibid.*   3, 190.
[77] *Ibid.*   3, 183.

to develop upward and become God: "Alles, was von Gott prädiziert wird, enthält die menschliche Zukunftslehre. . . Jeder Mensch, der jetzt von Gott und durch Gott lebt, soll selbst Gott werden."[78] Or again: "Gott will Götter."[79] This goal is reached through our moral will, which is God's will. Fulfilling his will we brighten and widen our existence, and as we develop this will we develop our insight and our power, "unser Wissen und Können," until when we have achieved morality we can do miracles, i.e.,—Novalis adds—"wo wir keine Wunder tun wollen, höchstens moralische."[80] In other words our individual will has become one with the world will,

To any reader of Novalis' poetry his pantheistic faith must be evident. In his aphorisms certain modifications, although these have also left their imprint on his verse, are more clearly apparent. God is the spirit that unites all, "der synkritische Geist"[81] as his romantic Kantian terminology phrases this idea. Here, too, the close interrelation between God and man is evident and Novalis plays with the etymology of *Gott* and *Gatt-ung*,[82] an etymology, which calls to mind Voltaire's saying about the science in which the consonants mean nothing and the vowels less. In Novalis' religion the idea of a *Mittler*, mediator, plays an important part. In a rather cryptic passage, which defends the idea that true religion is a union of pantheism anP monotheism, Novalis advances the thesis that everything can be "Mittler, Organ der Gottheit."[83] This pantheism is characterized by a pluralistic tendency: as the genius of the state reveals itself in every individual citizen, thus God reveals himself in a thousand varying forms in each religious body. "Der Staat und Gott, so wie jedes geistige Wesen, erscheint nicht einzeln, sondern in tausend mannigfaltigen Gestalten; nur pantheistisch erscheint Gott *ganz*, und nur im Pantheismus ist Gott *ganz*, überall, in jedem einzelnen." And again he voices in Fichtean terminology his belief in a development toward the absolute; he continues: "So ist für das grosse Ich das gewöhnliche Ich

[78] Novalis. 3, 358.
[79] *Ibid.* 2, 198.
[80] *Ibid.* 2, 290.
[81] *Ibid.* 3, 314.
[82] *Ibid.* 3, 274.
[83] *Ibid.* 2, 127 f.

und das gewöhnliche Du nur Supplemente. Jedes Du ist
ein Supplement zum grossen Ich. Wir sind gar nicht Ich,
wir können und sollen aber Ich werden. Wir sind Keime zum
Ich werden. Wir sollen alles in ein Du, in ein zweites Ich
verwandeln; nur dadurch erheben wir uns selbst zum grossen
Ich, das eins und alles zugleich ist."[84]

Of Novalis' lyric verse three poems need to be considered in
detail: *Hymnen an die Nacht*, the so-called *Hymne* of his *Geistliche
Lieder*, and *Gesang der Toten* in his novel *Heinrich von Ofterdingen*. The first of these is the direct expression of the poet's
grief over the death of Sophie von Kühn. Her death has taught
him that this life is death and that death is life. He celebrates
the night as the eternal mother of absolute life, the source of the
finite, herself infinite and eternal. Nowhere is the transcendental aspect of Novalis' affirmation of life so apparent as in these
hymns to the Night; he loves this world of light and gladly will
he stir his busy hands wherever he is needed and praise its
wondrous beauty, but his inmost heart belongs to the Night,
the realm of the absolute, the great beyond.

The second of these poems, often called *Die Abendmahls-
hymne*, seeks to explain the mystery of the sacrament. As the
lover thirsts for the lips of his loved one, longs to become one
with her, thus the believer seeks union with Christ in the com-
munion, to partake of His body and His blood. Let those who
would object to the use of sexual love as a religious symbol
please remember how closely interrelated sexual and religious
emotions are: modern psychology and modern literature are
in accord here. Novalis, by the way, was following out good
Christian tradition; I refer the reader to Moravian hymns and
the orthodox interpretation of the Song of Solomon as Christ,
the Bridegroom, seeking his Bride, the Church. The fundamental idea of the poem is that everything can be mediator
"Mittler, Organ der Gottheit." All will become one, the
eternal dualism of spirit and matter will be overcome:

> Einst ist alles Leib,
> Ein Leib,
> Im himmlischen Blute
> Schwimmt das selige Paar.

---

[84] Novalis. 2, 271.

"Das selige Paar" is of course the symbol of individual life merged in the unity of all life. In this sense the pluralistic monism of Novalis uses as its symbol the love of man and woman, the closest union in the finite world where two become one and still remain two. This pluralistic monism is even more marked in the *Gesang der Toten,* the supreme embodiment of Novalis' pantheistic faith. God is the ocean of life in which the souls of the departed are merged as drops and still retain their individuality. Thus there is a constant interplay and interaction between the individual and the All or God, and this the dead praise as their highest bliss.

> Süsser Reiz der Mitternächte,
> Stiller Kreis geheimer Mächte,
> Wollust rätselhafter Spiele,
> Wir nur kennen euch.
> Wir nur sind am hohen Ziele,
> Bald in Strom uns zu ergiessen,
> Dann in Tropfen zu zerfliessen
> Und zu nippen auch zugleich.
>
> Uns ward erst die Liebe Leben;
> Innig wie die Elemente
> Mischen wir des Daseins Fluten,
> Brausend Herz mit Herz.
> Lüstern scheiden sich die Fluten,
> Denn der Kampf der Elemente
> Ist der Liebe höchstes Leben,
> Und des Herzens eignes Herz.
>
> Zauber der Erinnerungen,
> Heil'ger Wehmut süsse Schauer
> Haben innig uns durchklungen,
> Kühlen unsre Glut.
> Wunden gibt's, die ewig schmerzen,
> Eine göttlich tiefe Trauer
> Wohnt in unser aller Herzen,
> Löst uns auf in eine Flut.
>
> Und in dieser Flut ergiessen
> Wir uns auf geheime Weise
> In den Ozean des Lebens
> Tief in Gott hinein;
> Und aus seinem Herzen fliessen
> Wir zurück zu unserm Kreise,
> Und der Geist des höchsten Strebens
> Taucht in unsre Wirbel ein.

HÖLDERLIN

Friedrich Hölderlin was born in 1770. His outward life is a struggle to gain a foothold, a means of sustenance, but inwardly he treads the bright Castalian brinks of beauty like John Keats, a worshipper at the shrine of ancient Greece, a dreamer after the ideal. Once he beheld this ideal, but—like all ideals— unattainable. It was Diotima, as he named her, the wife of the rich Frankfort banker in whose house he was private tutor. Too finely sensitive for this world of everyday trivialities and the endless struggle forced upon him, his wounded spirit shrouded itself in the darkness of insanity. This was in 1803. Forty years later he passed out of existence.

As a divinity student in Tübingen Hölderlin wrote in the autograph album of his friend Hegel the ancient Greek formula ἓν καὶ πᾶν. With Hegel he had studied Plato and Kant and with him he read Jacobi's *Letters on Spinoza*, a book which revealed Lessing's espousal of pantheism. With all his predi- lection for the beauty of Greek mythology, with all his Christian mysticism, Hölderlin was a pantheist all his days. The very poems, his last by the way, in which revealed Christian dogma is a most important factor, also give the fullest and clearest expression of his pantheistic faith. With his deep love of Nature, the Greek gods are to him symbolic embodiments of natural phenomena; the highest of all is "Vater Äther," the symbol of the poet's pantheistic deity. Hölderlin's conception of human freedom and his affirmation of life are largely influenced by his pantheism. While at the university and during the first subsequent years, Hölderlin is under the spell of Kant and Schiller and their idealism of freedom. A child of his time, he pays homage to the French Revolution—the Tübingen divinity students danced around a tree of liberty—and sings hymns to freedom. Still there is something transcendental about his conception of freedom, and even then the individual will is influenced by the collective will. Only a few years pass and the latter entirely takes the place of the former. Hölderlin was—spiritually speaking—an aristocrat, his oversensitive nature allowed him no other choice. When even his best work meets only deaf ears, he hurls out his defiant scorn in his own inimitable asclepiads; the mob likes only the loud things of the market place, and only the godlike believe in the godlike:

> Ach! der Menge gefällt, was auf den Marktplatz taugt,
> Und es ehret der Knecht nur den Gewaltsamen;
> An das Göttliche glauben
> Die allein, die es selber sind.
>
> *(Menschenbeifall)*

But in the very same year (1799) he writes his poem, *Stimme des Volkes*, in which he praises the voice of the people as the voice of God. As the people do not heed the wisdom of the poet, so do neither the flowing waters, and yet he loves to listen to them, as heedless of him they wander their predestined path to the ocean.

> Du seiest Gottes Stimme, so ahndet' ich
> In heil'ger Jugend; ja, und ich sag' es noch.—
> Um meine Weisheit unbekümmert
> Rauschen die Wasser doch auch, und dennoch
>
> Hör' ich sie gern, und öfters bewegen sie
> Und stärken mir das Herz, die gewaltigen;
> Und meine Bahn nicht, aber richtig
> Wandeln ins Meer sie die Bahn hinunter.

Thus Hölderlin does homage to the deep subconscious wisdom of the collective will, that unawares serves the cosmic goal. And yet he burns with the desire to change this unconscious and unwilling service into a service that sees its goal and rejoices in it. In his last poems, in *Hyperion* and *Empedokles*, he conceives this to be his prophet mission, and to his brother he wrote, June 4, 1799:

"Wir sind schon lange darin einig, dass alle die irrenden Ströme der menschlichen Tätigkeit in den Ozean der Natur laufen, so wie sie von ihm ausgehen. Und eben diesen Weg, den die Menschen grösstenteils blindlings, oft mit Unmut und Widerwillen, und nur zu oft auf gemeine unedle Art gehn, diesen Weg ihnen zu zeigen, dass sie ihn mit offenen Augen und mit Freudigkeit und Adel gehen, das ist das Geschäft der Philosophie, der schönen Kunst, der Religion, die selbst auch aus jenem Triebe hervorgehen."[85]

Hölderlin had drunk deep from the fountain of Greek antiquity and especially Greek tragedy. Closest akin he felt

---

[85] Hölderlin, Br. 493 f.

himself to Sophocles, his master, whose art he characterizes
thus in its innermost essence:

> Viele versuchten umsonst, das Freudigste freudig zu sagen,
> Hier spricht endlich es mir, hier in der Trauer, sich aus.
>
> *(Sophokles)*

Thus the Greek idea of fate did not remain to our poet a mere bit
of idle antiquarian lore; it is the embodiment of the moral law.
Even in those years when Hölderlin wrote his hymns to freedom
he believed that fate was a deciding factor, and in his hymn
Das Schicksal, written 1793, he lauded "eherne Notwendigkeit"
as the mother of all that is great and heroic, prefixing as a motto
a verse of Aeschylus that calls those wise that humbly do
homage to fate: προσκυνουντες την ειμαρμενην, σοφοι. After his
separation from Diotima the uncertainty of human existence
fills him with horror. The gods dwell in blessed peace, in
eternal serenity, but man in blind suffering is hurled through
the years into uncertainty as waters from cliff to cliff. This is
the burden of *Hyperions Schicksalslied:*

> Ihr wandelt droben im Licht
> Auf weichem Boden, selige Genien!
> Glänzende Götterlüfte
> Rühren euch leicht,
> Wie die Finger der Künstlerin
> Heilige Saiten.
>
> Schicksallos, wie der schlafende
> Säugling, atmen die Himmlischen;
> Keusch bewahrt
> In bescheidener Knospe
> Blühet ewig
> Ihnen der Geist,
> Und die seligen Augen
> Blicken in stiller
> Ewiger Klarheit.
>
> Doch uns ist gegeben
> Auf keiner Stätte zu ruhn,
> Es schwinden, es fallen
> Die leidenden Menschen
> Blindlings von einer
> Stunde zur andern,
> Wie Wasser von Klippe
> Zu Klippe geworfen,
> Jahrlang ins Ungewisse hinab.

More and more with mighty portent fate comes into the fore-
ground as a force that—heedless of individual wish and entreaty—
leads humanity to its destined goal. The individual must
bow to the law of organic development:

> Wie du anfingst, wirst du bleiben,
> So viel auch wirket die Not
> Und die Zucht, das meiste nämlich
> Vermag die Geburt
> Und der Lichtstrahl, der
> Dem Neugebornen begegnet.

In similar language Goethe expressed this same idea fifteen
years later in his poem Δαιμων. (*Urworte. Orphisch.* See above
p. 24.) The law of organic development rules the collective
whole as it rules the individual: everything is one unalterable
current of events, "ein Weltlauf unaufhaltsam." Least of all is
arbitrary freedom allowed to genius, the bearer of the divine
message. Hölderlin says of the Rhine, the symbol of genius:

> Unverständig ist
> Das Wünschen vor dem Schicksal.
> Die Blindesten aber
> Sind Göttersöhne, denn es kennet der Mensch
> Sein Haus, und dem Tier ward, wo
> Es bauen solle, doch jenen ist
> Der Fehl, dass sie nicht wissen wohin?
> In die unerfahrene Seele gegeben.

Thus the Rhine at first does not recognize its real purpose, to
serve Germany, the new land of promise; his longing drives him
to wander toward Asia, even as Hölderlin had ever sought
ancient Hellas—but the Alps force the self-willed stream to
wander his predestined path and fulfill his mission. The
Alps symbolize the eternally immovable powers of fate; they are
the mighty forge, wherein all pure things are shaped, "die
Esse, worin alles Lautre geschmiedet wird." But why do the
gods, why does the great cosmic all need the mortal individual?
Does not its own fulness suffice infinite life? The answer is:

> Es haben aber an eigner
> Unsterblichkeit die Götter genug, und bedürfen
> Die Himmlischen eines Dings,
> So sind's Heroen und Menschen,
> Und Sterbliche sonst. Denn weil

> Die Seligsten nichts fühlen von selbst,
> Muss wohl, wenn solches zu sagen
> Erlaubt ist, in der Götter Namen
> Teilnehmend fühlen ein andrer—
> Den brauchen sie.

There is a note here that reminds one of the later pantheism of Hegel and his school: only in the human spirit does the theistic principle attain to consciousness and really become God. Fichte had already expressed the same idea, but had made special mention of the will: God has his life in the human consciousness and will; he has no other. This seems to be the basis of Novalis' conception. We meet the same trend of thought in Richard Dehmel and more especially in the modern religious movement as exemplified by Arthur Bonus.

Hölderlin's affirmation of life results directly from his pantheism. His supreme faith is that all life is good, that joy is greater and more immortal than grief and woe. Even in his deepest suffering over the loss of Diotima, Hölderlin still holds to this faith. In *Menons Klage um Diotima*, Diotima brings to him the message for mankind that more immortal than care and anger is joy, and that each day ends in golden beauty:

> So bezeugest du mir's, und sagst mir's, dass ich es andern
> Wiedersage, denn auch andere glauben es nicht,
> Dass unsterblicher doch, denn Sorg' und Zürnen, die Freude
> Und ein goldner Tag täglich am Ende noch ist.

But even as early as 1794 the *Hyperion* fragment contains the passage: "Alles muss kommen, wie es kömmt. Alles ist gut." This is Hegel's later: "Was ist, ist vernünftig." In his last philosophic poem, *Patmos*, Hölderlin voices once more this same faith that all is good. He says of Christ, about to go to his death:

> nie genug
> Hatt' er, von Güte zu sagen,
> Der Worte damals, und zu erheitern, da
> Er's sahe, das Zürnen der Welt:
> Denn alles ist gut.

The closing paragraphs of Hölderlin's novel *Hyperion*, written only a few months after his separation from Diotima, give to us a fuller explanation of this faith:

"O Seele! Seele! Schönheit der Welt! du unzerstörbare! du entzückende! mit deiner ewigen Jugend! du bist: was ist denn der Tod und alles Wehe der

Menschen?—Ach! viel der Worte haben die Wunderlichen gemacht. Geschiehet doch alles aus Lust, und endet doch alles mit Frieden.

Wie der Zwist der Liebenden sind die Dissonanzen der Welt. Versöhnung ist mitten im Streit und alles Getrennte findet sich wieder.

Es scheiden und kehren im Herzen die Adern und einiges, ewiges, glühendes Leben ist alles."

These last words, that all is one glowing eternal life, give the keynote of the life work of Böcklin, Nietzsche and Dehmel. In Hölderlin's *Hyperion* the new optimism which recognizes suffering as an inherent factor in life has for the first time found its explanation in poetic form: "The discords of life are like the dissension of lovers. Reconciliation dwells in the midst of strife and all that is severed is again joined." The most gripping portrayal of the part that suffering plays in life the poet has given to us in his last poem *Patmos*. He describes the gamut of his own sufferings, how he had to leave his home, his friends—

furchtbar wahrhaft ist's, wie da und dort
Unendlich hin zerstreut das Lebende Gott.

He tells us how fate wrested Diotima from him, robbed him of his beauty, him whom his fellow students had likened to Apollo; how even his honor was attacked, the honor of the demigod—as he calls himself in rightful consciousness of his own worth—so that, beholding such suffering, the Highest averted his face; then the tormented individual rebels against this knowledge that all is good, and the question bursts from quivering lips: "Was ist dies?" And Hölderlin's answer is the most powerful symbol of the kind that I know:

Es ist der Wurf des Säemanns, wenn er fasst
Mit der Schaufel den Weizen
Und wirft den klaren zu, ihn schwingend über die Tenne;
Ihm fällt die Schale vor den Füssen, aber
Ans Ende kommet das Korn.
Nicht ihm ein Übel ist's, wenn einiges
Verloren gehet und von der Rede
Verhallet der lebendige Laut:
Denn göttliches Werk auch gleichet dem unsern,
Nicht alles will der Höchste zumal.

The spirit of the Universe is represented as a gigantic sower that
sifts his own being on a winnowing shovel.   And in this process,
of what matter is the individual and if he be a prophet?   Let
him perish, if but his message live.   Of him is spoken the word
of Nietzsche: "Was liegt an dir, Zarathustra?   Sprich dein
Wort und zerbrich."

WELTSCHMERZ

The poems of Hölderlin mark the summit of the romantic conception of life. If we compare Hölderlin with Novalis, we see that his philosophy is concerned more with this world, has an even deeper appreciation of suffering and stresses more definitely the limitation of human freedom. The later Romanticists we can pass by; their poetry, on the whole, is marked by a joyous optimism, but these poets, with the exception of Clemens Brentano, stay on the surface. For them life is not a problem, but a gift of God. And of Brentano it must be said that he is without any well-founded philosophy of his own: here and there he strikes pantheistic chords, but they never shape themselves into anything like a full symphony. Brentano is like a mirror that reflects the manifold fulness of life, but retains nothing. Thus Catholic dogma became the sole haven of refuge to his vacillating nature. It would be a highly profitable undertaking to show how the beginnings of an original poetical *Weltanschauung* are stifled by the rigidity of ecclesiastic doctrine. This study might be of interest for the art of the late Middle Ages and of the fifteenth and sixteenth centuries, where the same conflict was waged. Leaving Brentano, we pass over to the close of the Romantic period, to the poets of the so-called *Weltschmerz*. They belong to the generation that was born about 1800: Platen was born 1796, Heine 1797, and Lenau 1802. In their childhood they experienced the turmoil and the confusion of the Napoleonic Wars; in the years of youth, when the growing spirit craves freedom, their endeavors were stifled by the reactionary rule of Metternich. The great hopes, which the preceding generation had based on the French Revolution and the achievements of German poetry and philosophy, had come to naught. The romantic deification of the ego—this, strange to say, was Friedrich Schlegel's interpretation of Fichte, and it had gained wide acceptance—was followed by a bitter disillusion. Reac-

tion ruled in church and state.   Schleiermacher's great work
to found a freer Christianity had been forced into the background: within the church orthodoxy, withered and rationalis-
tic, held sway, and without a similar scepticism was developing.
Witness but Heine's scorn of "die Pfaffen des Atheismus"!
With all this the awakening of the natural sciences: Man learns
to look at life with disillusioned senses, the misery of existence
seems patent.   The earliest and at the same time fullest expression of this trend was Schopenhauer's *Die Welt als Wille und Vorstellung* (1818).   Strange to say the great philosopher of pessimism found no immediate hearing; he only came to his own
when a generation later the political ambitions of the thirties
and forties had come to grief, and weary of the strife engendered
by political and social discussions, mankind sought solace in the
metaphysics of pessimism. What the generation that during the
thirties and forties was imbued with a glowing zeal for political
and social reform thought of the philosophy of idealism can
best be shown by Heinrich Heine.   Why waste one's time on
metaphysics when people are begging for bread! When
Heine speaks of Kant and Schiller he fairly outdoes himself in
scorn and mockery, and the idealism of Fichte he counts among
the most colossal errors ever hatched by the mind of man. He
tells us it has achieved nothing for our social well-being; it is
of use only so far as it sets forth the utter fruitlessness of idealism in its final deductions and so far as it supplies the necessary
transition to the philosophy of Schelling.[86] Similarly Heine
denounces the transcendental idea of liberty as fruitless when he
says:

> Nur in der Tiefe des Gemütes
> Ein deutscher Mann die Freiheit trägt.
> (*Bei des Nachwächters Ankunft zu Paris*)

All of these poets join in the battle for political freedom; Platen
and Lenau are the impassioned champions of the Poles, Heine
sounds the note of social reform and considers himself to the
last the champion of liberty, as he had in the *Harzreise* introduced himself to the miner's daughter as the knight of the Holy
Spirit that frees mankind.   But for all this they chafe under

[86] Heine. 4, 262 f.

the narrowing fetters of fate and raise their voices in lament that
the individual is powerless in the clutches of the great All.

> Das Menschenherz hat keine Stimme
> Im finstern Rate der Natur,
>
> (*Aus!*)

Lenau complains, and Platen confesses in his odes, how futile
is our battle for freedom and knowledge:

> Stets um Freiheit buhlt das Gemüt, um Kenntnis;
> Doch um uns liegt rings, wie ein Reif, Beschränkung:
> Keine Kraft, selbst Tugend vermag der Zeit nicht
> Immer zu trotzen.
>
> (*Der bessere Teil*)

To be a finite creature is a curse, Platen tells us in one of his
earlier songs; to bury our pain in the oblivion of sleep is all we
can do:

> O suche ruhig zu verschlafen
> In jeder Nacht des Tages Pein;
> Denn wer vermöchte Gott zu strafen,
> Der uns verdammte Mensch zu sein!
>
> (*Du denkst die Freude festzuhalten*)

The poems of Platen (August Graf von Platen-Hallermünde,
born 1796, died in Syracuse, Sicily 1835), along with those of
Lenau are the purest expression of *Weltschmerz*. That wonderful translation of the choral ode from Oedipus on Kolonos
is born of Platen's own soul experience:

> Nicht gezeugt sein, wäre das beste Schicksal,
> Oder doch früh sterben in zarter Kindheit:
> Wächst zum Jüngling einer empor, verfolgt ihn
> Üppige Torheit,
>
> Während Missgunst, Streit und Gefahr und Hass ihm
> Quälend nahn; reift vollends hinan zum Greis er,
> Jede Schmach muss er dulden dann, vereinzelt
> Stehend und kraftlos.
>
> Stets umdrängt uns Flutengedräng und schleudert
> Hart an steilabfallenden Klippenstrand uns,
> Mag der Süd nun peitschen die Woge, mag sie
> Schwellen der Nordsturm.

The ancient tragic view of life that has found its consummate
expression in these verses of Sophocles is Platen's own: he

loved beauty and sought it with all the intense yearning of the artist; but his nature was hopelessly awry, he dreaded his own perverse desires, and so his yearning did not know the hope of fulfillment, but had to flee from it. To the world he was only a tool, from which it pressed forth song in thousandfold torment. Thus the deeper significance of Platen's *Tristan* reveals itself.

> Wer die Schönheit angeschaut mit Augen,
> Ist dem Tode schon anheimgegeben,
> Wird für keinen Dienst der Erde taugen,
> Und doch wird er vor dem Tode beben,
> Wer die Schönheit angeschaut mit Augen!
>
> Ewig währt für ihn der Schmerz der Liebe,
> Denn ein Tor nur kann auf Erden hoffen,
> Zu genügen einem solchen Triebe:
> Wen der Pfeil des Schönen je getroffen,
> · Ewig währt für ihn der Schmerz der Liebe.
>
> Ach, er möchte wie ein Quell versiechen,
> Jedem Hauch der Luft ein Gift entsaugen,
> Und den Tod aus jeder Blume riechen;
> Wer die Schönheit angeschaut mit Augen,
> Ach, er möchte wie ein Quell versiechen.

Thus the lament ever and ever again recurs in the varying forms that mark Platen's development as a poet: in the form of the oriental Ghasel, in numerous sonnets that are the finest in German literature, and in the odes that mark the summit of his artistry. I quote from the *Ghaselen:*

Es liegt an eines Menschen Schmerz und eines Menschen Wunde nichts,
Es kehrt an das, was Kranke quält, sich ewig der Gesunde nichts!
Und wäre nicht das Leben kurz, das stets der Mensch vom Menschen erbt,
So gäb's Beklagenswerteres auf diesem weiten Runde nichts!
Einförmig stellt Natur sich her, doch trausendförmig ist ihr Tod,
Es fragt die Welt nach meinem Ziel, nach deiner letzten Stunde nichts;
Und wer sich willig nicht ergibt dem ehrnen Lose, das ihm dräut,
Der zürnt ins Grab sich rettungslos, und fühlt in dessen Schlunde nichts;
Dies wissen alle, doch vergisst es jeder gerne jeden Tag,
So komme denn in diesem Sinn hinfort aus meinem Munde nichts!
Vergesst, dass euch die Welt betrügt, und dass ihr Wunsch nur Wünsche zeugt,
Lasst eurer Liebe nichts entgehn, entschlüpfen eurer Kunde nichts!
Es hoffe jeder, dass die Zeit ihm gebe, was sie keinem gab,
Denn jeder sucht ein All zu sein, und jeder ist im Grunde nichts.

Lenau

Nikolaus Niembsch von Strehlenau, famous under the name of Nikolaus Lenau, was born in Southern Hungary in 1802, died near Vienna after six years of insanity in 1850. Like Platen he seems predestined to be the poet of *Weltschmerz*. Over his life's gloomy journey—"die dunkle Erdenfahrt"[87]—one could place no more fitting motto than the verse from his *Faust:* "Die Sehnsucht nach dem Untergang"[88]—the yearning to perish. Faust, that symbol of the striving human soul, has to become the prey of Mephistopheles for Lenau, and the world seems to him, as he writes to a friend, a "res derelicta quae patet diabolo occupanti."[89] Once led astray by a youthful errant passion, a feeling of guilt, of innocence irretrievably lost, always haunts him and Dame Melancholy becomes his faithful life companion (*An die Melancholie*). When later on happiness in the guise of human love crosses his pathway, he does not dare stretch out his hand. Shuddering he feels that there is something too fatally abnormal about him that he should affix that heavenly rose to his gloomy dark heart.[90] Has happiness any reality?

> O Menschenherz, was ist dein Glück?
> Ein rätselhaft geborner,
> Und kaum gegrüsst verlorner,
> Nie wiederholter Augenblick.
>
> (*Frage*)

He lives in a veritable atmosphere of unhappiness and notes down with satisfaction the Homeric word ἀμφιμέλας as exactly describing his state.[91] If Lenau in his song tries to express a note of joy, a strangely artificial ring results. Even his power of poetic expression deserts him: at other times a master of poetic diction, he shows a lack of good taste; his metaphors lack reality, as when he calls the larks rockets of song hurled into the air by the exuberant youth Spring (*Der Lenz*), or when he lets the lark climb into the air "auf ihren bunten Liedern"

---

[87] Lenau. 2, 329.
[88] *Ibid.* 2, 120.
[89] *Ibid.* 4, 274.
[90] *Ibid.* 3, 92; 138.
[91] *Ibid.* 5, 150.

(*Liebesfeier*).   But let Lenau return to his atmosphere of grief
and his poetic imagery is of a most astounding reality:

> Der Buchenwald ist herbstlich schon gerötet
> So wie ein Kranker, der sich neigt zum Sterben,
> Wenn flüchtig noch sich seine Wangen färben.
> Doch Rosen sind's, wobei kein Lied mehr flötet.
>
> *(Herbstgefühl)*

Or when he compares the wind-tossed bush to a man sick of
soul, tossing restlessly on his couch; and the very rhythm
becomes a faithful reproduction of Nature:

> Wie auf dem Lager sich der Seelenkranke
> Wirft sich der Strauch im Winde hin und her.
>
> *(Himmelstrauer)*

The most powerful picture of lonely forsaken despair we find
in two sonnets entitled *Einsamkeit*—Solitude.   The first sonnet
describes how a human being, forsaken by God and love, alone
upon the waste heath, is driven to seek refuge with the rock
lying at his feet and clasps it in his arms, until frightened by the
dead solitude about him, he leaps to his feet and full of fear
stretches out his arms to the wind.   The second sonnet continues:

> Der Wind ist fremd, du kannst ihn nicht umfassen,
> Der Stein ist tot, du wirst beim kalten, derben,
> Umsonst um eine Trosteskunde werben,
> So fühlst du auch bei Rosen dich verlassen.
>
> Bald siehst du sie, dein ungewahr, erblassen,
> Beschäftigt nur mit ihrem eignen Sterben.
> Geh weiter: überall grüsst dich Verderben
> In der Geschöpfe langen, dunkeln Gassen:
>
> Siehst hier und dort sie aus den Hütten schauen,
> Dann schlagen sie vor dir die Fenster zu,
> Die Hütten stürzen, und du fühlst ein Grauen.
>
> Lieblos und ohne Gott!   der Weg ist schaurig,
> Der Zugwind in den Gassen kalt: und du?
> Die ganze Welt ist zum Verzweifeln traurig.

Towards the end of his gloomy pilgrimage on earth Lenau
comes to a more gentle and comprehensive view of things.
Reif sein ist alles.   He whose religious views had ranged from
Catholicism to utter scepticism now turns to pantheism and

there finds refuge. Nature gives to him as a parting boon that peaceful serenity of spirit that he had elsewhere sought in vain. The finest and ripest gift of Lenau's lyric art are his *Waldlieder*, written a year before insanity overtook him. He sees that suffering is justified and even recognizes it as a blessing. Like an errant child he returns to Nature and craves forgiveness for having sought elsewhere alleviation from suffering that she in her kindness gave him as bitter blessing. To the eternal dying in Nature he has become reconciled: it is not annihilation full of horror, but a silent sweet passing from state to state— "heimlich still vergnügtes Tauschen." Thus the *Waldlieder* end in a sweetly melodious autumn picture:

> Rings ein Verstummen, ein Entfärben:
> Wie sanft den Wald die Lüfte streicheln,
> Sein welkes Laub ihm abzuschmeicheln:
> Ich liebe dieses milde Sterben.
>
> Von hinnen geht die stille Reise,
> Die Zeit der Liebe ist verklungen,
> Die Vögel haben ausgesungen,
> Und dürre Blätter sinken leise.
>
> Die Vögel zogen nach dem Süden,
> Aus dem Verfall des Laubes tauchen
> Die Nester, die nicht Schutz mehr brauchen,
> Die Blätter fallen stets, die müden.
>
> In dieses Waldes leisem Rauschen
> Ist mir, als hör' ich Kunde wehen,
> Dass alles Sterben und Vergehen
> Nur heimlich still vergnügtes Tauschen.

HEINE

The development of Heinrich Heine (born 1797 in Düsseldorf, died 1856 in Paris, whither he had gone in 1831) is entirely different from that of Platen and Lenau. Only in certain phases of his life and work is he a representative of the *Weltschmerz;* a good part of his poetry has an utterly different ring, and the poet espouses the joys of the sensual world. While both Platen and Lenau, imbued with a strong metaphysical sense, made a sympathetic study of philosophy, Heine's excursions into this field are journalistic attempts to amuse the reader. As a Jew he is an outcast and is naturally drawn to the social problems

of the day, which Lenau barely touches upon and Platen never
mentions.   Like Platen and Lenau, however, Heine considers
himself all his life a champion of liberty and political freedom,
but is painfully aware of human helplessness, of the bounds of
human knowledge.   Thus the youth in the *Nordseebilder* tries
in vain to solve the riddle of life.   All religions and philosophies
have been of no avail, science is futile, Nature clothes herself
in scornful and ominous silence:

> Es murmeln die Wellen ihr ew'ges Gemurmel,
> Es wehet der Wind, es fliehen die Wolken,
> Es blinken die Sterne gleichgültig und kalt,
> Und ein Narr wartet auf Antwort.
>
> *(Fragen)*

The same accusation Heine hurls forth from his "mattress-
grave," his bed of torment, where for eight long years his life
was a slow death.   The poem is a veritable shriek of despair
at the fettered impotence of mortality:

> Lass die heil'gen Parabolen,
> Lass die frommen Hypothesen—
> Suche die verdammten Fragen
> Ohne Umschweif uns zu lösen.
>
> Warum schleppt sich blutend, elend,
> Unter Kreuzlast der Gerechte,
> Während glücklich als ein Sieger
> Trabt auf hohem Ross der Schlechte?
>
> Woran liegt die Schuld?   Ist etwa
> Unser Herr nicht ganz allmächtig?
> Oder treibt er selbst den Unfug?
> Ach, das wäre niederträchtig.
>
> Also fragen wir beständig,
> Bis man uns mit einer Handvoll
> Erde endlich stopft die Mäuler—
> Aber ist das eine Antwort?

But all this raging and gnashing of teeth is quite futile, even
our bitterest curse will not kill a fly:

> Ohnmächtige Flüche!   Dein schlimmster Fluch
> Wird keine Fliege töten.
> Ertrage die Schickung, und versuch
> Gelinde zu flennen, zu beten.
>
> *(Es hatte mein Haupt die schwarze Frau)*

These poems reveal the unrelieved pessimism which possessed Heine in his *Matratzengruft*. Till then Heine's attitude to life had passed through every possible stage, from the gloomy melancholy of youth to the most exuberant enjoyment of existence. Heine was egocentric to the highest degree, and so his attitude to life is entirely determined by his personal welfare. The poet's development in his *Buch der Lieder* (published in 1827) is the gradual yielding of the melancholy of youth to a more positive attitude to life; as he drinks in the sensual pleasures of existence his pessimism, being rather frail stuff, disappears. In the first cycle of *Das Buch der Lieder*, entitled *Junge Leiden*, the melancholy of the lovelorn youth moans; in the *Fresko-Sonette* his discontent with life and the world finds wrathful utterance. The two following cycles, *Lyrisches Intermezzo* and *Die Heimkehr*, mark the transition, and in the *Nordseebilder* Heine has attained a positive view of life. The end of the cycle is the poem *Im Hafen*, the very rhythm of which is drunk with life and wine.

> Glücklich der Mann, der den Hafen erreicht hat,
> Und hinter sich liess das Meer und die Stürme,
> Und jetzo warm und ruhig sitzt
> Im guten Ratskeller zu Bremen.

Neither Platen nor Lenau ever surrendered their pessimism thus readily. The gates of bliss are opened to him, where the twelve apostles, those casks full of sainthood, preach their silent, but eloquent sermon. Here he has a living proof, of what he always asserted, that the King of the Heavens does not live among quite common people, but in the very best of society. In this poem, as in *Die Götter Griechenlands*, Heine refutes the Christian ascetic ideal, and to the very end of his life he divides mankind into barbarians, i. e., the Jews and the Christians, the followers of the ascetic ideal, and Greeks ("Hellenen"), who believe in the beauty of the sensual world. Even on his bed of torment Heine still lauds the pleasures and the joy of the world which he is loath to leave. Gradually, however, a song of a different strain enters in and drowns out the more joyous notes. In the year 1839, when the first symptoms of disease came—Heine had had a premonition that he was marked by fate—he wrote those exquisitely simple and yet heart-rending verses entitled *Lass ab*.

> Der Tag ist in die Nacht verliebt,
> Der Frühling in den Winter,
> Das Leben verliebt in den Tod—
> Und du, du liebest mich!
>
> Du liebst mich—schon erfassen dich
> Die grauenhaften Schatten,
> All deine Blüte welkt,
> Und deine Seele verblutet.
>
> Lass ab von mir, und liebe nur
> Die heiteren Schmetterlinge,
> Die da gaukeln im Sonnenlichte—
> Lass ab von mir und dem Unglück.

In the same year he wrote his Song of Life, the greatest of his ballads: *Ritter Olaf*. Sir Olaf, who has enticed the king's daughter to illicit love, is condemned by the angered king to die at the close of the church ceremony. The newly wedded bridegroom asks for respite till midnight, and when according to his wish he has emptied the last cup and danced the last dance, smiling he goes to lay his head on the block and his red lips bless life, for lo, life was good.

> Ich segne die Sonne, ich segne den Mond,
> Und die Stern', die am Himmel schweifen.
> Ich segne auch die Vögelein,
> Die in den Lüften pfeifen.
>
> Ich segne das Meer, ich segne das Land,
> Und die Blumen, auf der Aue.
> Ich segne die Veilchen, sie sind so sanft
> Wie die Augen meiner Fraue.
>
> Ihr Veilchenaugen meiner Frau,
> Durch euch verlier' ich mein Leben,
> Ich segne auch den Holunderbaum,
> Wo du dich mir ergeben.

Through Sir Olaf Heine bids farewell to the life that he loved, the world of sensuous beauty. This love of the sensuous world has left its imprint on Heine's religious ideal. In the *Salon* he resounds the praise of Spinoza, whose pantheism he adapts and changes to suit his desires. Germany, he says, is the most propitious soil for pantheism: it is the religion of the greatest German thinkers and the best German artists, and deism in theory has long since perished in Germany. "Man sagt es nicht, aber jedermann weiss es; der Pantheismus ist das öffentliche Geheimnis in Deutschland. In der Tat, wir sind dem Deismus entwachsen. Wir sind frei und wollen keinen donnernden Tyrannen. Wir sind mündig und bedürfen keiner väterlichen Fürsorge. Auch sind wir keine Machwerke eines grossen Mechanikus. Der Deismus ist eine Religion für Knechte, für Kinder, für Genfer, für Uhrmacher. Der Pantheismus ist die verborgene Religion Deutschlands."[92] For this reason—Heine tells us—the disciples of Saint-Simon were better understood in Germany than in France, where materialism suppressed their system of thought.

This allusion to the school of Saint-Simon makes clear what attracted Heine to pantheism; it offers him the necessary metaphysical background for the glorification, the canonization of sensual life, the emancipation of the flesh, to use a phrase of the time. God and Nature, body and soul, spirit and matter, all only one inseparable substance. Also in his political and social lyrics Heine is an apologist of the material world, as for instance in his advice to the German people not to allow themselves to be put off with promises of a future Paradise, where angels will cook heavenly rapture without butcher's meat, but to fill their stomachs with the good things of this earth (*Erleuchtung*). Or his poem *Doktrin:*

> Schlage die Trommel und fürchte dich nicht
> Und küsse die Marketenderin!
> Das ist die ganze Wissenschaft,
> Das ist der Bücher tiefster Sinn.

The best poetical expression of Heine's pantheism as a canonization of the life of the senses is contained in his cycle *Seraphine*, especially the seventh poem.

> Auf diesem Felsen bauen wir
> Die Kirche von dem dritten,
> Dem dritten neuen Testament:
> Das Leid ist ausgelitten.

---

[92] Heine. 4, 224.

Vernichtet ist das Zweierlei,
Das uns so lang betöret:
Die dumme Leiberquälerei
Hat endlich aufgehöret.

Hörst du den Gott im finstern Meer?
In tausend Stimmen spricht er.
Und siehst du über unserm Haupt
Die tausend Gotteslichter?

Der heil'ge Gott, der ist im Licht
Wie in den Finsternissen;
Und Gott ist alles, was da ist;
Er ist in unsern Küssen.   ·

This sensuous pantheism, however, was of little avail, when, to quote Heine's own words, God Jehovah showed him his clawing vultures, and—having for a long time herded swine with the disciples of Hegel—he gave up his pantheism and returned to God like the Prodigal Son.[93]   The life of the senses had lost all its allurements, yes, the senses themselves had died and the faith that canonized them had become an idle meaningless mockery.   And now existence, at least his existence, sometimes all existence, fills him with despair and becomes a curse.   The emptiness of life and the knowledge of the frailty of all things here was the theme of an earlier poem, which the melancholy Lenau prized above all.

Es ragt ins Meer der Runenstein,
Da sitz' ich mit meinen Träumen.
Es pfeift der Wind, die Möwen schrein,
Die Wellen, die wandern und schäumen.

Ich habe geliebt manch schönes Kind
Und manchen guten Gesellen—
Wo sind sie hin?   Es pfeift der Wind,
Es schäumen und wandern die Wellen.

To some extent this poem expresses a doubt in the value of existence.   All is transitory, all is vanity: ceaseless change in ceaseless monotony, ceaseless monotony in ceaseless change, is the message that the very form of the poem embodies.   We do not have, however, that shrill despair that admits of no alleviation till we come to the *Romanzero* (published 1851) and the

---

[93] Heine. 1, 485. Strodtmann. 2, 376.

Last Poems. And what could one expect in them? Not able to move, racked by almost incessant pains, only his spirit painfully alive, Heine embodies in these poems such agonies as no poet ever endured. Heine himself said to Alfred Meissner about these poems: "Das ist schön, entsetzlich schön! Es ist eine Klage wie aus einem Grabe, da schreit ein Lebendigbegrabener durch die Nacht, oder gar eine Leiche, oder gar das Grab selbst. Ja, solche Töne hat die deutsche Lyrik noch nie vernommen und hat sie auch nicht vernehmen können, weil noch kein Dichter in solch einer Lage war."[94] The main theme of the *Romanzero* is summed up in two verses, variations of which recur again and again like a Leitmotif:

> Und das Heldenblut zerrinnt
> Und der schlechtere Mann gewinnt.
> *(Walküren)*

Or to quote one of the very last poems:

> das ist das Los,
> Das Menschenlos:—was gut und gross
> Und schön, das nimmt ein schlechtes Ende.
> *(Es kommt der Tod.)*

The entire book of *Historien,* the first of the *Romanzero,* is an embodiment of this idea: the meaner man wins, and good is turned into destructive evil. This is brought to its terrible climax: kings and beggars, poets and harlots, the very Gods themselves are swept along into this maelstrom of destruction. The rightful king is conquered by the invading bastard; in gruesome vision we see Marie Antoinette at a morning *lever* headless in her circle of court ladies, likewise without heads: the poet Firdusi, basely deceived by his king, dies of starvation; Pomare, the dancing queen of the demimonde, is resuced from her loathsome fate by a timely death; beauty can only be saved from the world's defiling pollution by killing it; Apollo, the God of Music, becomes a Jewish rake travelling through the lands with a retinue of nine wenches as an itinerant actor; and Vizliputzli, the Mexican God, turns into a devil to become, as syphilis, the scourge of Europe. Thus Heine sees in life and in history the tendency to perdition. And yet, in spite of

---

[94] Strodtmann, 2, 392.

all this, the will to life holds him in its clutches and forces him to cling to this frightful existence: give up everything, fame, happiness, honor, only live, breathe, "nur leben, atmen, schnaufen" (*Epilog*). Only seldom a note is heard that rises to purer spheres of harmony, that breathes something of the peace of renunciation, as in the wonderful verses that describe Sleep and his sterner and nobler brother Death; the former with his wreath of poppies has often assuaged his pain for a time, but only the latter can bring him full recovery.

> Gut ist der Schlaf, der Tod ist besser, freilich
> Das Beste wäre nie geboren sein.
> (*Morphine*)

And yet this suffering was to Heine a bitter blessing. Only in this sheer superhuman battle with suffering did the singer of sweet songs become a world-poet; here his life becomes truly heroic. His suffering he makes a plastic circumstance, subservient to his art. Two weeks before his death he wrote his poem *Für die Mouche*, that mysterious woman who cheered his last months of agony and brought a halo of love to his death-bed. Whoever compares the love elegy in this poem to the earlier love lyrics cannot but see how Heine's love of woman has been spiritualized; here woman is a spiritual entity, not primarily corporeal. Suffering has purged the poet of his grosser elements, it was the mighty forge in which all pure things are shaped, "die Esse, in der alles Lautere geschmiedet wird," to quote again the beautiful words of Hölderlin. Heine's *Gedanken und Erinnerungen*, published after his death, contain the following observation: "Im Christentume kommt der Mensch zum Selbstbewusstsein des Geistes durch den Schmerz —Krankheit vergeistigt, selbst die Tiere."[95]

---

[95] Heine. 7, 404.

REALISM AND A NEW FAITH IN LIFE

While Heine in his mattress grave was defying and cursing fate, a more realistic poetry was voicing the joy of life. Take, for example, Eduard Mörike (1804-1875): his idylls breathe the pleasure of everyday life, in his song the waters at midnight still sing of the beauty of the day. In art a similar trend is apparent in the paintings of Moritz von Schwind and Ludwig Richter. The tragic note is by no means absent in Mörike's poems. It once seemed as if the fate of Hölderlin would overtake him; the odes addressed to Peregrina reflect this struggle. This crisis passed, Mörike's aim was to achieve sweet content, avoiding all excess of joy and grief. Thus he attained in a smaller sphere the harmony that was Goethe's, whom he revered as his master. But he lacked the latter's intellectual greatness and keenness. His gentle soul, free from all deeper metaphysical wants, was content to live his simple religion of the heart. A more intense struggle for metaphysical insight is evident in Gottfried Keller and Friedrich Hebbel.

KELLER

Gottfried Keller was born in Zürich in 1819, died there in 1898. For many years he served his city as *Stadtschreiber* (municipal clerk). Of sturdy Swiss peasant stock he is a child of this Earth, singularly objective and free from all sentimentalism. Under the influence of Ludwig Feuerbach, whom he heard lecture in Heidelberg in 1848, he cast aside his belief in a personal God. The chief tenet of Feuerbach is *Homo homini deus*. The verse of Genesis that God created man in His likeness Feuerbach changes to: man always created God in the likeness of man. God, as the symbol of infinite perfection, is only an ideal created by mankind. Thus mankind can also annul this deity and replace it by a new ideal. In this way the whole responsibility for the shaping of the race rests within the hands of man. This is like an anticipation of Nietzsche, only that Nietzsche emphasizes more clearly the evolutionary prin-

ciple, the development upward from man to *Übermensch*.
With Feuerbach, Keller rejects the belief in personal immortality. Why should man occupy an exceptional place in this
scheme of things? All else perishes, why not he? In days of
gloomy despair Keller gave up his belief in personal immortality; in his life's calm maturity he sees that he has done right.

> Ich hab' in kalten Wintertagen,
> In dunkler hoffnungsarmer Zeit
> Ganz aus dem Sinne dich geschlagen,
> O Trugbild der Unsterblichkeit.
>
> Nun, da der Sommer glüht und glänzet,
> Nun seh' ich, dass ich wohlgetan;
> Ich habe neu das Herz umkränzet,
> Im Grabe aber ruht der Wahn.
>
> Ich fahre auf dem klaren Strome,
> Er rinnt mir kühlend durch die Hand;
> Ich schau' hinauf zum klaren Dome—
> Und such' kein besseres Vaterland.
>
> Nun erst versteh' ich, die da blühet,
> O Lilie, deinen stillen Gruss,
> Ich weiss, wie hell die Flamme glühet,
> Dass ich gleich dir vergehen muss.

Under the influence of these views the world, Keller writes,
becomes "klarer, strenger, aber auch glühender und sinn-
licher."[96] The thought of death enhances the value of life,
it impels man to make the fullest use of his earthly opportuni-
ties. "Das Leben ist wertvoller und intensiver, der Tod ern-
ster, bedenklicher und fordert mich nun erst mit aller Macht
auf, meine Aufgabe zu erfüllen, und mein Bewusstsein zu
reinigen und befriedigen, da ich keine Aussicht habe, das
Versäumte in irgend einem Winkel nachzuholen."[97] Death ever
drives the wise man into life and teaches him to act, Goethe
says in *Hermann und Dorothea;* the premonition of death makes
Hebbel realize the fulness of life (*An den Tod*); the same idea
Böcklin seems to express in his portrait of himself with fiddling

[96] Ermatinger. 2, 185.
[97] *Ibid.* 2, 275.

death looking over his shoulder.   Compare also this poem of
Keller:

> Wir wähnten lange recht zu leben,
> Doch fingen wir es töricht an;
> Die Tage liessen wir entschweben
> Und dachten nicht ans End' der Bahn.
>
> Nun haben wir das Blatt gewendet
> Und frisch dem Tod ins Aug' geschaut;
> Kein ungewisses Ziel mehr blendet,
> Doch grüner scheint uns Busch und Kraut!
>
> Und wärmer ward's in unserm Herzen,
> Es zeugt's der froh gewordne Mund;
> Doch unsern Liedern, unsern Scherzen
> Liegt auch des Scheidens Schmerz zu Grund.

Death has assumed a new meaning for Goethe, Hebbel, Keller,
and Böcklin.   Death is no longer the arch enemy of man,
but only a necessary factor of existence and even a means to
enrich life.   The song no longer is: in the midst of life we are in
death; but rather, in the midst of death we are in life.   Death
ends only individual existence, the race lives on, and the life of
the race takes the place of personal immortality in another
sphere for Keller as for Feuerbach.   When Heine died, Keller
noted down on the margin of his *Apotheker von Chamounix*, a
longer poem, in which he had made light of Heine's deathbed
conversion: "Der Tod des einzelnen tötet nicht, aber der Tod
aller."[98]   A man that has lived his life has no fear of death;
he is content to live on in the race and does not long for personal
immortality.   This seems to be the idea of Keller's *Wochen-
predigt:*

> Im heissen Glanze liegt die Natur,
> Die Ernte lagert auf der Flur;
> In langen Reihn die Sichel blinkt,
> Mit leisem Geräusch die Ähre sinkt.

This is Nature's silent and eloquent sermon on the mystery of
life and death: the ripe grain is garnered.   But within the
church we have another scene: there the parson is toiling
through his weekly sermon and is expounding to his flock of
aged peasant folk, that have had their goodly fill of life, the

---

[98] Dünnebier, H. 94.

doctrine of immortality.   And after the sermon—such is the
irony of life—our friend the parson, who was so anxious to
give to his listeners all eternity for steadfast endeavor, dozes off
in sleep for lack of better means of using to advantage a single
afternoon.   His peasants, however, who have worked and
struggled and toiled, and have also drained their full portion of
life's joys, know no other desire than to rest forever.   The service over, they sit about the churchyard, their final resting
place, while through the fields of ripening grain wander their
sturdy sons with their wives and children, the present and
the future generation, the symbol of life eternal.   Keller's
frohe Diesseitigkeit has its roots in this faith.   When he passed
his seventieth birthday, Conrad Ferdinand Meyer wrote to
him: "Weil Sie die Erde lieben, wird die Erde Sie auch so
lange als möglich festhalten."[99]   Of Keller's love of life there
is no finer expression than his *Abendlied*, one of the very few
lyric poems of his later years.   The aging poet is walking over
the evening fields eager to drink in to the last life's overflowing
golden beauty.

> Augen, meine lieben Fensterlein,
> Gebt mir schon so lange holden Schein,
> Lasset freundlich Bild um Bild herein:
> Einmal werdet ihr verdunkelt sein!
>
> Fallen einst die müden Lider zu,
> Löscht ihr aus, dann hat die Seele Ruh;
> Tastend streift sie ab die Wanderschuh,
> Legt sich auch in ihre finstre Truh.
>
> Noch zwei Fünklein sieht sie glimmend stehn
> Wie zwei Sternlein innerlich zu sehn,
> Bis sie schwanken und dann auch vergehn,
> Wie von eines Falters Flügelwehn.
>
> Doch noch wandl' ich auf dem Abendfeld,
> Nur dem sinkenden Gestirn gesellt;
> Trinkt, o Augen, was die Wimper hält,
> Von dem goldnen Überfluss der Welt.

With all his optimistic faith Keller is deeply conscious of the
inherent tragedy of existence.   With all its beauty life is cruel,
relentlessly cruel, as for example in *Romeo und Julia auf dem*

---

[99] C. F. Meyers Briefe. 1, 307.

Dorfe, Keller's masterpiece in the field of the short story.   How deeply akin the poet feels to all suffering creatures is shown by *Die kleine Passion*.   The mellow September breeze wafts a small winged creature upon the volume of verse he is perusing; it is seeking a shroud and a resting place.   Not to disturb its last moments the poet leaves the volume open.

> So liess den Band ich aufgeschlagen
> Und sah erstaunt dem Sterben zu,
> Wie langsam, langsam ohne Klagen
> Das Tierlein kam zu seiner Ruh'.
> Drei Tage ging es müd' und matt
> Umher auf dem Papiere;
> Die Flügelein von Seide fein
> Erglänzten alle viere.
> Am vierten Tage stand es still
> Gerade auf dem Wörtlein "will!"
> Gar tapfer stand's auf selbem Raum,
> Hob je ein Füsschen wie im Traum;
> Am fünften Tage legt' es sich,
> Doch noch am sechsten regt' es sich,
> Am siebten endlich siegt' der Tod,
> Da war zu Ende seine Not.
> Nun ruht im Buch sein leicht Gebein,
> Mög' uns sein Frieden eigen sein!

This, Witkop remarks in his *Neuere deutsche Lyrik,* the average man might be tempted to compare with Hans Sachs in its love of detail painting.   "But," he continues, "what a world-development, what a sea of human endeavor and human suffering is surging between the two.   How unspeakably must humanity, how unspeakably must a human being have suffered to become so free, so kindly, so all-loving, so all-affirming.   Here one must recall Keller's word to Nietzsche, that it is great pain that makes man more eloquent."[1]   Keller too avows that suffering is a blessing, he admires the clear logical consistency of the just measure given him, which he will quaff with thirsting lips.

> Ich kenne dich, o Unglück, ganz und gar
> Und sehe jedes Glied an deiner Kette!
> Du bist vernünftig, zum Bewundern klar,
> Als ob ein Denker dich geordnet hätte!
>
> Nicht mehr nicht weniger hat mir gebührt,
> Mir ist gerecht die Schale zugemessen;

[1] Witkop. 2, 306.

Und dennoch hab' ich bittrer sie verspürt,
Als niemals ich getrunken noch gegessen.

Jetzt aber bring' ich leichter sie zum Mund,
Als einst die müde Seele noch wird wissen;
Der quellenklare Perltrank ist gesund,
Ich lieb' ihn drum mit dürstendem Gewissen.

The final poem of the cycle, *In der Trauer*, is most characteristic for Keller's unassuming and austere attitude so utterly free from all sentimental self-glorification. Suffering is not given to us as a mark of distinction, but as a lesson. The sun on high laughs at the little chap that struts along in his self-woven cloak of grief, the crown of thorns upon his brow, and thus put to shame, he lays both down by the wayside.

Conrad Ferdinand Meyer has called joy and sorrow "ein Geschwisterpaar, unzertrennlich beide." This also is the view of Keller; suffering steels and purges, joy ennobles, both are the gifts of Heaven to its beloved. This is the message of Keller's *Herbstlied*.

Wohl wird man edler durch das Leiden
Und strenger durch erlebte Qual;
Doch hoch erglühn in guten Freuden,
Das adelt Seel' und Leib zumal.
Und liebt der Himmel seine Kinder,
Wo Tränen er durch Leid erpresst,
So liebt er jene drum nicht minder,
Die er vor Freuden weinen lässt.

Und sehnen blasse Gramgenossen
Sich nach dem Grab in ihrer Not,
Wem hell des Lebens Born geflossen,
Der scheut noch weniger den Tod!
Taucht euch ins Bad der Lust, ins klare,
Das euch die kurze Stunde gönnt,
Dass auch für alles heilig Wahre
Ihr jede Stunde sterben könnt.

HEBBEL

Friedrich Hebbel (born in Dithmarschen in 1813, died in Vienna in 1863) was of a more metaphysical bent than Keller. With intuitive insight and brooding reflection he strove to solve the final questions of existence. His own bitter experiences left their indelible imprint on his views and yet were not able to warp them, for the poet and thinker rose above his narrow lot and viewed life as a whole. Dire need and suffering, privations and galling restrictions form the dark story of the first thirty-three years of Hebbel's life. Thus the unsurmountable barriers of all human endeavor force themselves on him with the result that he denies the freedom of the will. March 2, 1842, Hebbel writes in his diary: "Der Mensch hat freien Willen—d. h., er kann einwilligen ins Notwendige." And again, December 21, 1851: "Die sogenannte Freiheit des Menschen läuft darauf hinaus, dass er seine Abhängigkeit von den allgemeinen Gesetzen nicht kennt." These words do not so much indicate a Titan-like rebellion of the individual as the recognition of the moral law that controls the Universe. For on the 19th of October 1839, Hebbel had written in his diary: "Die Schranke der Kreatur ist die Freiheit der Natur," i. e., the freedom of Nature presupposes the limitations of the individual. Similarly, May 1, 1840: "Die Notwendigkeit der Schöpfung ist die Grenze menschlicher Freiheit," i. e., human liberty is limited by the moral necessity of the Universe. Thus genius, although free from all outer compulsion, is held in restraint. "Das Genie ist in seiner höchsten Freiheit gebunden, das forzierte Talent kann, was es soll," i. e., genius can only accomplish what is inherent in it and thus obeys the law of organic development, while the more or less artificial talent can execute whatever task is imposed from without (January 29, 1840). Thus in his sonnet to art Hebbel declares that his is no wilful sacrifice; he fought to maintain his freedom, but art won the battle:

> Dir, heil'ge Kunst, dir hab' ich mich ergeben!
> Nicht drängt' ich mich, du riefst mich zum Altare,
> Ich rang mit dir, ob ich mich frei bewahre,
> Du siegtest, nimm mich denn auf Tod und Leben.
>
> (*An die Kunst*)

Hebbel sees that necessity and moral law coincide. Humanity, however, can only shape itself in the most bitter struggle and the fetters are often crushing. Seeing injustice prevail Hebbel bids defiance to a moribund social order that chokes with its established rights and privileges the freer forms of life to whom the future rightfully belongs. Thus Hebbel, as later on Ibsen, becomes the accuser of the prevailing order;

its chief fault is that it has outlived its usefulness and to hold its own it must stifle ruthlessly all new life. A specific instance of this Hebbel has embodied in his *Maria Magdalene*, a tragedy of modern everyday life; the more general aspects of the problem we meet in the sonnet *Die menschliche Gesellschaft.*

> Wenn du verkörpert wärst zu einem Leibe,
> Mit allen deinen Satzungen und Rechten,
> Die das Lebendig-Freie schamlos knechten,
> Damit dem Toten diese Welt verbleibe;
>
> Die gottverflucht, in höllishem Getreibe,
> Die Sünden selbst erzeugen, die sie ächten,
> Und auf das Rad den Reformator flechten,
> Dass er die alten Ketten nicht zerreibe:
>
> Da dürfte dir das schlimmste deiner Glieder,
> Keck, wie es wollte, in die Augen schauen,
> Du müsstest ganz gewiss vor ihm erröten!
>
> Der Räuber braucht die Faust nur hin und wieder,
> Der Mörder treibt sein Werk nicht ohne Grauen,
> Du hast das Amt, zu rauben und zu töten.

This sonnet, however, is not a defense of arbitrary revolution and frenzied attempts at reform. It was written on the second of September, 1841. Two days later the sonnet, *Der Mensch und die Geschichte* gives another aspect of the same problem: individual and humanity as a whole. The poet represents history as a mighty sculptress that is hewing from brittle and unyielding material the pure image of mankind. The individual must perish that the ideal of humanity may come to life. But as we watch the sculptress at her task we ever tend to mistake the fragments that she has discarded for the divine image she strives to attain:

> Die Weltgeschichte sucht aus spröden Stoffen,
> Ein reines Bild der Menschheit zu gestalten,
> Vor dem, die jetzt sich schrankenlos entfalten,
> Die Individuen vergehn, die schroffen.
>
> Die endliche Vollendung ist zu hoffen,
> Denn diese Künstlerin wird nie erkalten,
> Auch sehen wir, wenn sich die Nebel spalten,
> Schon manchen Zug des Bildes tief getroffen.

Doch wir, wie Kinder in der Werkstatt harrend,
Wir haschen nach den abgesprungnen Stücken,
Die, wie sie schweigend meisselt, niederfallen.

Dann rufen wir, in Andacht dumpf erstarrend,
Mit krummen Nacken und gebeugten Rücken:
"Hier sind die Götter, lasst den Weihrauch wallen!"

The individual is ever a part of a greater whole, and if he
would attain his destined measure of perfection he cannot
seclude himself, but must in joy and in suffering surrender his
inmost self to the tumultuous ocean of life.   Thus he will find
himself: "Der Weg zu dir führt eben durch das Ganze" and serve
himself and serve the world-plan (*Welt und Ich*).   Neither need
man dream that he can change the course of the world by his
arbitrary endeavor.   Everything is a part of one unalterable
whole, and who would stem this tide will only destroy himself. Compare the sonnet *Die Freiheit der Sünde:*

O glaube nicht, dass du durch deine Sünde
Die Welt verwirrst!   Wie du auch freveln mögest,
Und ob du Gott dein Ich auch ganz entzögest,
Du hinderst nicht, dass sie zum Kreis sich ründe!

Ja, ob du, in des Innern Abgrunds Schlünde
Hinunter taumelnd, völlig dich betrögest
Und dich hinauf zur Götterfreiheit lögest,
Doch trifft dich das Gericht, das ich verkünde!

Wir leben nur im Ewigen und Wahren,
Und ihm entfliehen wollen, würde heissen,
In unsrer Brust den Odem anzuhalten;

Wir können's, doch es wird sich offenbaren,
Dass wir das eigne Lebensband zerreissen
Und nichts dadurch im Äther umgestalten.

This sonnet was written in Naples in 1845.   In his art Hebbel
was gradually overcoming the implacable tragic element in his
own life.   Only a few years later the effect of this change is
clearly visible in his dramas.   In his earlier tragedies no conciliatory note, no ray of a future hope, penetrates the utter
gloom; into all his later tragedies there falls the softening light
of a possible solution, of a reconciliation to be attained at a
future day.   This is Hebbel's final step to an unqualified
affirmation of life, clearly expressed already in the above sonnet.

Hebbel's whole previous development tended in this direction, his attitude to life was never negative. In hours of dark despair he might feel his own personal lot as curse, but his own grief and suffering never made him doubt in life as a whole. The suffering individual—what is he that he should defile the eternal beauty of the world with his grief?

> Und musst du denn, trotz Kraft und Mut,
> An jedem Dorn dich ritzen,
> So hüt' dich nur mit deinem Blut
> Die Rosen zu bespritzen.

Joy had been an all too rare visitor in Hebbel's life, as is shown by his prayer to the goddess of fortune for the lonely drop on the brim of her cup, whose full measure had gone to others (*Gebet*). Joy he felt as something holy, as something that is God's own.

> Uns dünkt die Freude Altarwein,
> Am Heiligsten ein sünd'ger Raub;
> Zieht Gottes Hauch durch unser Sein,
> So fühlen wir uns doppelt Staub.
> (*Es grüsst dich wohl ein Augenblick.*)

And the thought that suffering is a mark of distinction, that it proves you to be one of God's elect, ever bore him up. Nietzsche once remarked that a man's worth could be determined by the amount of suffering he had borne or was able to bear. Thus Hebbel wrote in 1839:

> Geht stumm an dir vorbei die Welt,
> So fühle stolz und andachtsvoll:
> Ich bin ein Kelch für Gott bestellt,
> Der ihn allein erquicken soll.

The poems quoted or alluded to above are with the single exception of the Prayer taken from the cycle, *Dem Schmerz sein Recht* (To Pain its Due). The title, added in 1857 when Hebbel gathered these poems into a group, is an expression of the final harmony won. The cycle contains poems that are the outcry of most intense anguish; their only consolation is that even in destruction harmony is Nature's eternal law. On the other hand the cycle proves how early Hebbel balanced the final account. In 1841 he wrote the tenth poem, where with still bleeding wounds he blesses pain:

Unergründlicher Schmerz!
Knirscht' ich in vorigen Stunden,
Jetzt mit noch blutenden Wunden
Segnet und preist dich mein Herz.

When his solitude in Paris (1845) was further embittered by the grief for the death of his son, no prayer for deliverance struggles forth from his heart, but in deep humility he recognizes the eternal validity of Nature's laws. His soul is thirsting and yearning for annihilation, but his prayer only asks that he may be awakened last of all creatures from the deep slumber which his spirit craves. It is clearly evident that grief had readier access to Hebbel than joy. This seems to be the privilege of mortals that are more finely attuned than the average. "Prosperity, pleasure, and success, may be rough of grain and common in fibre, but sorrow is the most sensitive of all created things." Thus Oscar Wilde wrote from *Reading Gaol*. Sorrow is not only most sensitive, but it makes sensitive. But in considering Hebbel let us not forget how his whole suppressed being was eager to burst out in joyous rapture at the slightest opportunity. When in his poverty stricken gloomy student days at Munich there came a little ray of cheer (his faithful friend Elise Lensing had sent him a new coat) he wrote his spring song:

Ringt um des Jubels Krone!
Das ist das Weltgebot.
Die trunkenste der Seelen
Wird Gott sich selbst vermählen
Durch sel'gen Freudentod.

There is, however, a strained note in these songs of joyous rapture: they are not so deeply embedded in Hebbel's very nature as his songs of grief. And must not the allusion to death as the acme of joy have its deeper significance? One is reminded how Klara in *Maria Magdalene* has an oppressing sense of guilt because in all the beauty of approaching summer she can only feel her own bitter misery, or how Agnes Bernauer trembles at her full cup of happiness. Hebbel did not attain to his absolute affirmation of life without a struggle, but finally the victory was his. As he adjudged to suffering its rightful sphere in life, so he also praised illness in his later days, because it alone leads to that quiet pleasure of existence that knows neither wish nor necessity:

Krankheit, dich auch lob' ich und preis' ich.   Zur reinen Freude am Dasein,
Welche nicht wünscht noch bedarf, bist du der einzige Weg.

Death itself is but a part of life's beauty:

Alles wird uns Genuss, so schön ist das Leben gerundet,
Selbst der Tod, denn der Schlaf ist der genossene Tod.

Thus life rounds itself into a perfect ring and it becomes a haven of peace.   Few poems breathe a deeper peace than Hebbel's *Herbstbild.*

Dies ist ein Herbsttag, wie ich keinen sah!
Die Luft ist still, als atmete man kaum,
Und dennoch fallen raschelnd fern und nah
Die schönsten Früchte ab von jedem Baum.

O stört sie nicht, die Feier der Natur!
Dies ist die Lese, die sie selber hält,
Denn heute löst sich von den Zweigen nur,
Was vor dem milden Strahl der Sonne fällt.

In the last days of his life Hebbel had his little daughter read Schiller's *Spaziergang* to him; then he said: "Der grosse heilige Mann!   Stets hat das Schicksal geflucht, und stets hat Schiller gesegnet."   As this word is true of Schiller, it is true of Hebbel. His poetic last will and testament is the poem *Der Bramine*, written during the final months of suffering, "in schweren Leiden," as the poet wrote below the finished manuscript.   The poem tells how a holy man in India, a Brahmin, is tempted in vain to have his suffering pass into another creature, however lowly, and thus gain surcease from his pangs.   He will not wrong any creature, not even the snake that strikes its venomous fangs into his body.   Greater love beareth no man.   As reward of such virtue Brahma frees him from all suffering and calls him to his side.   Thus the tragic poet confesses himself akin to all creatures, even the lowliest, in suffering and in love.[2]

---

[2] Witkop.   2, 256.

PESSIMISM

A not very distant future will probably recognize in Friedrich Hebbel the world's supreme tragic genius since Shakespeare, more purely tragic indeed than the greater English dramatist. Only in the dramas of Aeschylus and Sophocles has such a consistently tragic view of life found embodiment before Hebbel. Attic tragedy owes its totality of conception to its religious significance. It seeks a solution for the awful mystery of fate and human existence, tries to reveal it in symbols of suffering and the final answer is a resigned: "We do not know and cannot know, but Apollo, the God knows."[3] Hebbel's tragedy attains this totality of view: tragic guilt and life are enmeshed into one inseparable union, tragedy and tragic suffering form the *sine qua non* of all human progress and endeavor. This is the basic idea of Hebbel's tragic art, and this —so closely akin are contending opposites—must needs lead to a positive valuation of life. When Hebbel introduces into his later dramas the outlook upon a future reconciliation, he takes the first step of overcoming through tragedy itself the tragic view of life. The world, however, did not seem ready for this solution and absolute pessimism became the prevailing view of life. Schopenhauer now reaped a full measure of recognition. The second edition of *Die Welt als Wille und Vorstellung* appeared in 1844, the third in 1859, and the fourth in 1874. In this work and in the more popular *Parerga und Paralipomena* (1851) the poets of pessimism found their metaphysical background. One and all they drank deep at the fountain of their master and acknowledged him as such as also did Richard Wagner. Eduard Grisebach (1845-1906) wrote a biography of Schopenhauer and edited the first critical edition of his works. Hieronymus Lorm (pseudonym for Heinrich Landesmann 1821-1902) wrote a book entitled *Der grundlose Optimismus* (1874), the very title inspired by Schopenhauer. Pantheism had become pansatanism, the ultimate possible development of

---

[3] Wilamowitz. 1, 10-15.

pessimism. The torments and pangs of existence may rend us and tear us, may fill us with despair, but the will to life holds us in its clutches and makes forever impossible our deliverance in Nirvana. This doctrine of Schopenhauer Grisebach puts into verse in *Der neue Tannhäuser* (1869). The book is a reinterpretation of the old Tannhäuser motif, the ancient conflict between the carnal joys of Venus and the asceticism of Christ. Grisebach takes over the old symbols and fills them with new meaning. Sexual desire, woman as the tempting embodiment of Satan, ever lures us away from our only salvation, the peace of cosmic death. Non-existence is the real and only God, Satan is the will to life.

> Ihr fragt verzweifelnd: was ist Gott?
> Was nicht die Welt ist, das ist Gott!
> Das selige Nichts, die Todesruh—
> O schliesst das Auge der Dinge zu!
>
> Wir aber haben Wachs in den Ohren,
> Wir sind des Teufels schwachköpfige Toren,
> Er will und immer sagen wir: ja!
> Und die leidende Welt steht noch immer da.
>
> Ja, unser Wille, ohne Zweifel,
> Das ist die Welt, das ist der Teufel:
> Zögst du den alten Adam aus,
> So ginge die Weltgeschichte nach Haus;
>
> So stünde still das Rad der Natur,
> So wäre die Flamme der Kreatur
> Gedämpft und ausgelöscht ihr Wehe—
> Indessen, der Wille der Menschheit geschehe!
>
> Sie träumt ja gern den grossen Traum
> Noch immer fort in Zeit und Raum,
> Und ewig hängt am Kreuz vergebens
> Der tote Gott des ewigen Lebens.

The verse of Hieronymus Lorm is of a far higher poetical value. It is less sicklied o'er with the pale cast of thought, since it is born of the poet's own experience. Suffering all his days, deaf and partially blind since his fifteenth year, later totally blind and paralyzed so that the ordinary channels of communication with the outside world were cut off, Lorm sees that to live and to suffer are identical. The beautiful Greek myth of the harmony of the spheres becomes to the stricken poet a questioning lament about the meaning of life.   Why does the Universe teem with life, why were we awakened from non-existence?

SPHÄRENGESANG

So lang' die Sterne kreisen
Am Himmelszelt,
Vernimmt manch Ohr den leisen
Gesang der Welt:
"Dem sel'gen Nichts entstiegen,
Der ew'gen Ruh',
Um ruhelos zu fliegen—
Wozu?   Wozu?"

Human freedom is naught but a deception and a delusion; thus the leaf that is borne along by the whirlwind boasts of its wings.

MENSCH UND SCHICKSAL

Das Schicksal ist ein Wirbelwind,
Ein armes Blatt das Menschenkind.
Er treibt's zu Tal, er hebt's zum Hügel—
Das Blättchen rühmt sich seiner Flügel.

Life is naught but suffering and guilt and the pain of parting; this is all that our eye will see.   To the evanescent dream of love and happiness life grants only space sufficient to perish. This is *Weltlauf:*

Wohin das Auge dringt,
Ist Schuld und Leiden
Und was der Zeitlauf bringt,
Ist Fliehn und Scheiden.

Da zwischen hat der Traum
Von Glück und Liebe
Nur noch so viel an Raum,
Dass er zerstiebe.

Schopenhauer's famous maxim about the relative percentage of joy and suffering in life Lorm translates into verse, and under the caption *Fromme Bücher* he directs his shafts against the pious that would make us believe that the world is an offspring of a Heavenly Father's kindly grace and love.

Aus Gottes Herzen ist die Welt entsprungen,
Als seiner Liebe, seiner Huld Erscheinung!

So spricht die Katze, wenn ihr Fang gelungen—
Die Maus doch ist nicht ganz der gleichen Meinung.
Zwar täglich kommt ein frommes Buch heraus,
Doch nirgends fand ich widerlegt die Maus.

And immortality, a prolongation of existence beyond the grave, how can one desire that, believe that? Lorm's only wish, when he has been borne beyond the churchyard wall, is to be conscious of a deep feeling of rest, to know thus that it is over.

DAS LETZTE ZIEL

Ich glaub' nicht an die Dauer
Jenseits der Kirchhofmauer.
Doch wünsch' ich nur so viel
Mir als das letzte Ziel,
Wenn abgetan des Lebens Last
Zu fühlen eine tiefe Rast.

But with all his suffering, with his firm conviction that life is only pain and grief and heartache, a senseless ray of hope will not leave his stricken soul. The generalizing reflective epigram of Pope:

Hope springs eternal in the human breast,
Man never is, but ever to be blessed.

Lorm may not have known, but the insight Pope had thus expressed our poet had gained, and he translates it into the living breath of experience.

Und droht auch Nacht der Schmerzen ganz
Mein Leben zu umfassen—
Ein unvernünft'ger Sonnenglanz
Will nicht mein Herz verlassen.

Since pessimism had become the predominant view of life and swayed all philosophic and religious creeds, the poetry of pessimism presents a marked variety of hues and colors. Beside the pure Schopenhauerian atheism of Grisebach and Lorm we find the Christian mysticism of Prinz Emil von Schönaich-Carolath (1852-1909), whom one might call a Christian disciple of Lord Byron. His first volume of verse bore the characteristic title *Lieder an eine Verlorene* (1878). His *Dichtungen* were published in 1883. A marked predilection is apparent for the great sinners, Don Juan, Faust, Ahasuerus, Judas, in whose views of life, love, and woman the poet's study of Schopenhauer is clearly evident. Woman to them is the fair Lucifer that forever betrays; (to Carolath himself as to Goethe the eternal feminine, *das Ewig-Weibliche*, is the saving principle of Divine Grace). And love, this passion against which man is powerless, the old physician—in a longer poem *Die Sphinx*—who has fathomed life with keenest insight, calls the epileptic dance of mankind, "der Menschheit Veitstanz." Life he characterizes as a mad endeavor to quench the desires that consume us.

> Des Weltalls dunkler Zug
> Ist das Verlechzen, und es lechzt, wer lebt.
> Das Leben ist ein grosser Wanderflug
> Nach der Begierden endlicher Erfüllung
> Und was die Welt erschüttert und durchbebt,
> Der Notschrei ist's nach tiefer Durstesstillung.

Under this dark law Carolath's heroes live. Only in Heaven beyond, if attained, is there release for them as for his Don Juan, whom the love of a pure woman purges and saves. A few quotations will show us Carolath's own view. Unfulfilled longing alone makes life possible:

> Nichterfüllung nur,
> Des grossen Wunsches Nichterreichen bildet
> Die Lebensmöglichkeit.
>
> *(Die Sphinx)*

Pain and longing lead us heavenward:

> In jedem Herzen zittert ein Magnet,
> Der rastlos sich zur ew'gen Heimat dreht.
> Ein Weg, daran mit kurzer Pause
> Der Schmerz als Meilenzeiger steht,
> Führt rasch nach Hause.
>
> *(Sang des Türmers)*

Carolath's inmost belief is best summed up in his *Albumblatt*. Again we hear that renunciation is our heaven-willed destiny.

> Hab' nicht zu lieb die knospende Rose:
> Es flöge gar bald
> Ohn' Heimat, ohn' Halt
> Ihr Duft Dir vorüber ins Uferlose.
>
> Unsterblich ist Schmerz allein.
> Was nie Du bebessen,

Ersehnt, nie vergessen,
Wird Deines Himmels Grundbau sein.

* * *

Den Daseinsfrohen, den emsig Lebenden,
Am Alltagskleide rüstig Webenden
Gehört die Welt mit goldnen Halmen.
Doch jene, die fröstelnd in Lebensmitten
An Sehnsucht, an Schwermut, an Heimweh gelitten,
Krönt erst der Tod mit Friedenspalmen.

The title of Carolath's first volume of verse *Lieder an eine Verlorene* is significant for the whole epoch; it was probably suggested by Ada Christen's *Lieder einer Verlorenen*, published in 1868. The content of Grisebach's *Der neue Tannhäuser* belongs to the same general tendency, and a similar title we have again in Hermann Conradi's (1862-1890) *Lieder eines Sünders*. Conradi too is a disciple of Schopenhauer. Identifying himself with the so-called modern movement he becomes the most relentlessly naturalistic of the poets of pessimism.

His *Lieder eines Sünders* (1887) picture the *taedium vitae*, the loathing of existence, which was the natural result of the wave of materialism that swept over the new empire in the eighties. The mad race for material advancement, against which Carolath raised his voice in solemn warning, intensified the already prevailing pessimism. Life became without meaning and content. Greed and lust, lust and greed alone urge man on. The time of great heroes, of men with inspired vision, Conradi tells us, is gone. We are a race of pigmies that burn incense to empty idols; the creative impulse is dead and deadly routine rules.

Was wir vollbringen, tun wir nach Schablonen,
Und unsre Herzen schrein nach Gold und Dirnen,
Und keinen gibt's, der tief im Herzen trüge
Den Hass, der aufflammt gegen diese Lüge—
Wir knien alle vor den Götzen nieder
Und singen unserer Freiheit Sterbelieder.

(Pygmäen)

Thus the heart is filled with the sense of the meaninglessness of existence and is gripped convulsively by loathing. There is no relief but the dreamless sleep of death. This is Conradi's final word on life in his poem *Tiefste Qual*.

THE NEW OPTIMISM

NIETZSCHE

The decade from 1880-1890 marks the high tide of pessimism and materialism. In literature the prevalence of naturalism with its emphasis on the petty and the sordid is but another aspect of the same phenomenon. It must not be forgotten, however, that naturalism was primarily a revolt against a pseudo-classic *Schönfärberei* and worship of the mock heroic. This revolt of the naturalists was not without its heroic aspect; they fought a brave fight to attain a truer and greater art. The heroic impulse was by no means dead. This decade marks the beginning of a reawakened deeper interest in Kleist and Hebbel. Conrad Ferdinand Meyer wrote his historical *Novellen*. Conradi himself, even his verse proves that, was thirsting for the heroic and voiced his belief in a greater future. "Des bin ich gewiss," he wrote in 1884, "wir stehen schon im Frührot der grossen Bewegung."[4] He had already come under the spell of the prophet of the new idealism and optimism, around whose standard the younger generation were soon to flock in ever greater numbers. I refer to Friedrich Nietzsche. To live is to strive, life's sole purpose and aim is an ever higher development. This is the sum and substance of Nietzsche's new gospel as it is the message of his own heroic life. Nietzsche walked to the end of the road that Hebbel set out upon—to conquer the tragic view of life through tragedy itself. What he achieved was—to quote Witkop—"die Überwindung der Tragik durch den Tragiker, die Bejahung des Lebens aus tragischer Erkenntnis, trotz tragischer Erkenntnis, eben um der tragischen Erkenntnis willen."[5] To return to the optimism of the eighteenth century was manifestly impossible after Schopenhauer and Darwin, after Kleist, Hebbel, and Wagner. Mankind had gained too deep an insight into the tragedy of existence. As Nietzsche puts it: "Unser Zeitalter hat sich neue Augen

---

[4] Conradi. 2, 237.
[5] Witkop. 2, 355.

eingesetzt, um überall das Leiden zu sehen und mit einer ungeheuren hypnotischen Starrheit des Blicks, die nur einmal bisher in der Geschichte ihres Gleichen hatte, das Auge des Beschauers in die gleiche Richtung zu zwingen."[6] The prophet of the new optimism had himelf experienced deeply the heart breaking horrors of existence, he makes Goethe's phrase "am Leben leiden" his own. "Furchtbar ist das Alleinsein mit dem Richter und Rächer des eignen Gesetzes . . . Schreien wirst du einst: ich bin allein."[7] These words of Zarathustra voice Nietzsche's own tragic experience, the curse of the abysmal solitude that has ever been the lot of the prophet and seer. To his young friend Heinrich von Stein Nietzsche wrote in 1882: "Ich sage Ihnen aufrichtig, dass ich selber zu viel von dieser 'tragischen' Komplexion im Leibe habe, um sie nicht oft zu verwünschen. . . . Da verlangt es mich nach einer Höne, von wo aus gesehen das tragische Problem *unter* mir ist. Ich möchte dem menschlichen Dasein etwas von seinem herzbrecherischen und grausamen Charakter nehmen."[8] The way of the creative spirit, Zarathustra tells us, is full of suffering and the bitterness of death: "Wahrlich, durch hundert Seelen ging ich meinen Weg und durch hundert Wiegen und Geburtswehen. Manchen Abschied nahm ich schon, ich kenne die herzbrechenden letzten Stunden." This path, however, leads to deliverance, for it was of his own choosing; he willed it thus. Zarathustra continues: "Aber so will's mein schaffender Wille, mein Schicksal. Oder, dass ich's euch redlicher sage; solches Schicksal gerade—will mein Wille."[9] Thus the proud self-determination of Fichte and Schiller once more appears, and, strange to say, Schopenhauer has led the way. Under the influence of Darwin, Nietzsche re-interprets Schopenhauer's doctrine of the will. For the philosopher of pessimism the will was blind, aimless, purposeless, unless its purpose and aim be to force man and all living things to cling to the curse of existence. Nietzsche's will has an aim and a purpose; man's evolution upward from man to superman. This is the meaning of Nietzsche's will to power, it is

[6] Witkop. 2, 355.
[7] Nietzsche. 6, 92.
[8] *Ibid.* Br. 3, 182.
[9] *Ibid.* 6, 125.

the will to evolution. The incarnate principle of this will is the
Übermensch, whose sole purpose and desire is to raise man to a
higher level.   Thus new vistas of higher possibilities loom up
and once more the triumphant song of life bursts forth.   Even
the most abject of all creatures, the ugliest man, exclaims:
"War Das—das Leben, will ich zum Tode sprechen.   Wohlan!
Noch Ein Mal!"[10]   The doctrine of eternal recurrence is born
out of this love of life.   Zarathustra lauds life in *Das trunkene
Lied* because of its infinite possibilities of joy and grief.   And
grief passes away, but joy is eternal.

> O Mensch!   Gib Acht!
> Was spricht die tiefe Mitternacht?
> "Ich schlief, ich schlief—,
> Aus tiefem Traum bin ich erwacht:—
> Die Welt ist tief,
> Und tiefer als der Tag gedacht.
>
> Tief ist ihr Weh—,
> Lust—tiefer noch als Herzeleid:
> Weh spricht: Vergeh!
> Doch alle Lust will Ewigkeit—,
> Will tiefe, tiefe Ewigkeit!"

It must be borne in mind that the *Übermensch* is a racial
ideal. Nietzsche makes the highest excellence of society his
ethical end. This excludes all arbitrary wilfullness and Nietzsche
differentiates between *Wille* and *Willkür* as Goethe.   The
individual may give its imprint to thousands; Zarathustra
yearns to imprint his hand upon the centuries as upon bronze,
but the real will can only find expression in the will to evolution.
All else is mere arbitrary whim and leads to self-annihilation.
Zarathustra teaches that all life in its innermost essence is
obedience.   "Wo ich nur Lebendiges fand, da hörte ich auch die
Rede vom Gehorsame.   Alles Lebendige ist ein Gehorchendes.
Und dies ist das Zweite: Dem wird befohlen, der sich nicht
selber gehorchen kann.   So ist es des Lebendigen Art.   Dies
aber ist das Dritte, was ich hörte: dass Befehlen schwerer ist,
als Gehorchen.   Und nicht nur, dass der Befehlende die Last
aller Gehorchenden trägt, und dass leicht ihn diese Last zer-
drückt:— Ein Versuch und Wagnis erschien mir in allem Be-

---

[10] Nietzsche. 6, 462.

fehlen; und stets, wenn es befiehlt, wagt das Lebendige sich selber
dran.   Ja noch, wenn es sich selber befiehlt, auch da noch muss
es sein Befehlen büssen.   Seinem eignen Gesetze muss es
Richter und Rächer und Opfer werden."[11]

This obedience includes willingness for self-sacrifice.   Goethe,
Fichte, Hölderlin, and Nietzsche all teach this same fundamental truth; renounce thyself for thy work.   In his lectures
Über die Bestimmung des Gelehrten Fichte says: "Ich bin
dazu berufen, der Wahrheit Zeugnis zu geben; an meinem Leben
und meinen Schicksalen liegt nichts; an den Wirkungen meines
Lebens liegt unendlich viel."   Thus Zarathustra can say of
himself: "Trachte ich nach meinem Glücke?   Ich trachte
nach meinem Werke."[12]   Unwilling to take the burden of the
new message upon himself, fearing that it may crush him,
Zarathustra hears the terrible words of the most silent hour:
"Was liegt an dir, Zarathustra?   Sprich dein Wort und zerbrich."[13]   It is the message of Nietzsche's own life.   His
motto was: "Wenn Denken dein Schicksal ist, so verehre dies
Schicksal mit göttlichen Ehren und opfere ihm das Beste, das
Liebste."[14]   This is the spirit of his poem *Ecce homo*.

> Ja, ich weiss, woher ich stamme,
> Ungesättigt gleich der Flamme
> Glühe und verzehr' ich mich.
> Licht wird alles, was ich fasse,
> Kohle, alles, was ich lasse,
> Flamme bin ich sicherlich.

Is this poem not a rebirth of Goethe's *Selige Sehnsucht?*   Not
that I mean to impute any conscious adaptation; these poems
are born of a similar experience, of the same view of life with a
faith in evolution.   Nietzsche's is more intensely personal,
egocentric, filled with the pathos of self-sacrifice; Goethe's is
more general and breathes the peace of full maturity.

> Sagt es niemand, nur den Weisen,
> Weil die Menge gleich verhöhnet,
> Das Lebend'ge will ich preisen,
> Das nach Flammentod sich sehnet.

---

[11] Nietzsche.   6, 166 f.
[12] *Ibid.*   6, 476.
[13] *Ibid.*   6, 216.
[14] *Ibid.*   11, 20.

In der Liebesnächte Kühlung,
Die dich zeugte, wo du zeugtest,
Überfällt dich fremde Fühlung,
Wenn die stille Kerze leuchtet.

Nicht mehr bleibest du umfangen
In der Finsternis Beschattung,
Und dich reisset neu Verlangen
Auf zu höherer Begattung.

Keine Ferne macht dich schwierig,
Kommst geflogen und gebannt,
Und zuletzt, des Lichts begierig,
Bist du, Schmetterling, verbrannt.

Und solang' du das nicht hast,
Dieses: Stirb und werde!
Bist du nur ein trüber Gast
Auf der dunklen Erde.

Nietzsche's entire endeavor is characterized by a deep religious fervor: the ideal of the *Übermensch* and the doctrine of eternal recurrence bear evidence of this. In religion as in all life two fundamental questions are of vital concern: the individual ego and its valuation, and the Universe or the Deity. The religious systems of the past have with but few exceptions found their answer to the first question in the belief of a continuance of personal existence after death. For Nietzsche personal immortality exists only in the doctrine of eternal recurrence.[15] Aside from this man continues to live only in the race as a link in an endless chain. Thus the intensely individualistic philosophy of Nietzsche has a pronounced collectivistic aspect. In the first aphorism of *Die fröhliche Wissenschaft*, Nietzsche defends the maxim: "Die Art ist Alles, Einer ist immer Keiner,"[16] and in the same book he calls the denial of the individual Schopenhauer's cardinal mistake.[17] Thus, we see the *Übermensch* is both an individual and racial ideal. The immortality of the race with its evolution upward from man to superman takes the place of personal immortality.

---

[15] Nietzsche. 5, 265.
[16] *Ibid.* 5, 34.
[17] *Ibid.* 5, 131.

But what of Nietzsche's conception of the Deity? At the age of eighteen Nietzsche wrote the poem *Dem unbekannten Gott.* He pledged himself to the service of the unknown God.

> Noch einmal, eh ich weiter ziehe
> Und meine Blicke vorwärts sende,
> Heb' ich vereinsamt meine Hände
> Zu dir empor, zu dem ich fliehe,
> Dem ich in tiefster Herzenstiefe
> Altäre feierlich geweiht,
> Dass allezeit
> Mich Deine Stimme wieder riefe.
> Darauf erglüht tiefeingeschrieben
> Das Wort: Dem unbekannten Gotte.
> Sein bin ich, ob ich in der Frevler Rotte
> Auch bis zur Stunde bin geblieben:
> Sein bin ich—und ich fühl die Schlingen,
> Die mich im Kampf darniederziehn
> Und, mag ich fliehn,
> Mich doch zu seinem Dienste zwingen.
> Ich will Dich kennen, Unbekannter,
> Du tief in meine Seele Greifender,
> Mein Leben wie ein Sturm Durchschweifender,
> Du Unfassbarer, mir Verwandter!
> Ich will Dich kennen, selbst Dir dienen.

Nietzsche kept his vow. Arthur Bonus has said that the religion of the future would perhaps not use the word God; it had become meaningless, having been used of such varied conceptions. So different have these conceptions been that the cry of atheism has always been raised against the new church by the old. Nietzsche cast aside not only the word but all former conceptions of the Deity. None the less Nietzsche has probably more than any other force influenced the modern religious movement in Germany. I would refer to Albert Kalthoff's *Zarathustrapredigten* and to the works of Arthur Bonus, especially *Religion als Schöpfung.* Creative idealism, man as the creator, is the essence of the last named work. What is it to have religion? Nietzsche answers: "Religion haben heisst dem Leben einen ewigen Sinn geben, mitten im Endlichen das Unendliche fühlen und besitzen." These words remind one of Schleiermacher's definition of immortality.

"Mitten in der Endlichkeit Eins werden mit dem Unendlichen und ewig sein in jedem Augenblick, das ist die Unsterblichkeit der Religion."[18]   This similarity of view is not accidental.   It shows how intensely vital Romanticism is and presages perhaps undreamed of future developments.   Nietzsche shapes a new ideal for mankind; for the old unattainable ideal of a God he substitutes a new ideal that is attainable, *der Übermensch.* Like an evening sky aglow with future glory he hung over mankind the word of great noon-day, "das Wort vom grossen Mittage," when the will of all will say: "Tot sind alle Götter, nun wollen wir, dass der Übermensch lebe."[19]   The old nobility that looks into the past, he replaces by a new nobility that looks into the future, the love of the land of our fathers by the love of the land of our children.   "Euer Kinder Land sollt ihr lieben: diese Liebe sei euer neuer Adel,—das unentdeckte im fernsten Meere.   Nach ihm heisse ich eure Segel suchen und suchen."[20]

The whole trend of development in the nineteenth century is towards this creative idealism.   This ideal of the Deity was to a certain extent formulated already by Hölderlin, more clearly by Fichte and Hegel and the Hegelians: that God only attains to self-consciousness in the human spirit, only there really becomes God.   In Nietzsche it has received its ultimate possible development, man is the creator and he creates the world as he wills it.

"Wollen befreit: das ist die wahre Lehre von Wille und Freiheit—so lehrt sie euch Zarathustra.

Nicht-mehr-wollen und Nicht-mehr-schätzen und Nicht-mehr-schaffen! ach, dass diese grosse Müdigkeit mir stets ferne bleibe!

Auch im Erkennen fühle ich nur meines Willens Zeuge—und Werdelust; und wenn Unschuld in meiner Erkenntnis ist, so geschieht dies, weil Wille zur Zeugung in ihr ist.

Hinweg von Gott und Göttern lockte mich dieser Wille; was wäre denn zu schaffen, wenn Götter—da wären!

Aber zum Menschen treibt er mich stets von neuem, mein inbrünstiger Schaffens-Wille; so treibt's den Hammer hin zum Steine.

Ach, ihr Menschen, im Steine schläft mir ein Bild, das Bild meiner Bilder! Ach, dass es im härtesten, hässlichsten Steine schlafen muss!

---

[18] Schleiermacher, *Reden über die Religion* (Hendel) **106.**
[19] Nietzsche.   6, 115; 289.
[20] *Ibid.*   6, 297.

Nun wütet mein Hammer grausam gegen sein Gefängnis. Vom Steine
stäuben Stücke: was schiert mich das?

Vollenden will ich's: denn ein Schatten kam zu mir—aller Dinge Stillstes
und Leichtestes kam einst zu mir!

Des Übermenschen Schönheit kam zu mir als Schatten. Ach, meine Brü-
der! Was gehen mich noch—die Götter an!"[21]

DEHMEL

The pantheistic conception of the Universe has left its imprint
upon German literature from Goethe and the Romantic poets
to the present.   The reader will recall Hölderlin's symbol of
the spirit of the Universe as a mighty sower winnowing his own
being.   In Dehmel's epic poem *Zwei Menschen* we have the
same symbol.   Lea and Lux, the two lovers, are wandering in
winter through the silent forest.

> Und der Wald schweigt, wie von Andacht gepackt;
> Der erste Schnee liegt tief und schwer.
> Aus Höfen und Scheunen vom Talgrund her
> Tönt gedämpft der Dreschertakt.
> Fern, gross im weissen Sonnenglast
> Steht eine Bäuerin und worfelt Korn;
> Zuweilen blitzt ihr Sieb auf wie voll Zorn,
> Dann flattern Spatzen.   Der Mann macht Rast:
> "Dieses Schauspiel ergreift mich immer,
> Als sei's der Mutter Menschheit Bild.
> Da steht das riesige Frauenzimmer,
> Ihre Worfel schüttelnd, wild, schaffenswild,
> Die Körner hütend mit harten Tatzen
> Vor Eifer glühend, vor Freude rot:
> Tanzt auch manch leichtes zu den Spatzen,
> Die schweren geben Menschenbrot."[22]

The idealistic pantheism of Hölderlin and Hegel has assumed a
naturalistic aspect.   The symbol, however, clearly shows that
humanity is more than the mere sum of the individuals com-
posing it, just as a people, a nation, is more than the aggregate
sum of its individual members.   Thus, also, Nature is more than
the aggregate sum of its individual phenomena.   There is a
mysterious unifying force in Nature that welds all things into
one, all individual life is bound together.   The sacred stillness
of early morning reveals to the poet the unity of Nature.

---

[21] Nietzsche.   6, 125 f.
[22] Dehmel.   5. 166.

MORGENANDACHT

Sehnsucht hat mich früh geweckt;
Wo die alten Eichen rauschen,
Hier am Waldrand hingestreckt,
Will ich Dich, Natur, belauschen.

Jeder Halm ist wie erwacht;
Grüner scheint das Feld zu leben,
Wenn im kühlen Tau der Nacht
Warm die ersten Strahlen beben.

Wie die Fülle mich beengt!
So viel Grosses! so viel Kleines!
Wie es sich zusammendrängt
In ein übermächtig Eines!

Wie der Wind im Hafer surrt,
Tief im Gras die Grillen klingen,
Hoch im Holz die Taube gurrt,
Wie die Blätter alle schwingen,

Wie die Bienen taumelnd sammeln
Und die Käfer lautlos schlüpfen—
Oh Natur! was soll mein Stammeln,
Seh ich all das Dich verknüpfen:

Wie es mir ins Innre dringt,
All das Grosse, all das Kleine,
Wie's mit mir zusammenklingt
In das übermächtig Eine!

God is for Dehmel the all uniting principle of the world, the great all-pervading rhythm. Even the Greek ἓν καὶ πᾶν the poet embodies in a symbol of concrete vividness that shows how all is one in mystic unity.

Aus des Abends weissen Wogen
Taucht ein Stern;
Tief von fern
Kommt der blasse Mond gezogen.

Tief von fern
Aus des Morgens grauen Wogen
Langt der grosse blasse Bogen
Nach dem Stern.
             (*Tief von fern*)

The conscious element in the Universe is man. The human spirit, when in a moment of inspiration it suddenly sees clearly into what was deepest mystery, is the revealing medium of the cosmic All.

ERLEUCHTUNG

Plötzlich wird, was dunkel war,
Dir von Grund aus offenbar;
Und dann kannst du nicht verstehen,
Dass du sonst es nicht gesehen.

Aus dem Grund der Welt durch dich
Offenbart die Welt es sich;
Aus der Ewigkeit geboren
Bleibt es ewig unverloren.

In this way the doctrine of Hegel and his school and the faith of Hölderlin recur. Out of this faith is born the same humanism that we have in Feuerbach and Nietzsche. Primitive man, in the childhood of the race, created the gods and worshipped them as the creators of all things. Later on, man sees that what he worshipped as the creation of the Gods is the work of mankind.

HEIDNISCHER GLAUBE

Als der kindliche Mensch noch seinen Träumen vertraute
Und dem luftigen Raum luftige Wesen ersann,
Als sein Sehnen die Freiheit, die keinem Irdischen glückte,
Einem himmlischen Volk schenkte mit betender Hand:
Da verlieh er den Bildern des Traums ein leibhaftiges Leben,
Auf dem erstrittenen Herd thronte der ruhige Gott.
Seinem seligen Wahn entwuchs die beglückende Schönheit;
Weil er edel geirrt, wurde ein Edleres wahr.
Wo er die Gottheit geglaubt, da hatte die Menschheit gewaltet;
Glaub an die Menschheit, Mensch, und sie befreit dich zum Gott.

This faith does not lead to vaunting arrogance, but to a deep feeling of humility. Individual man is born of the great world and is thus a created thing, the work of God. Let man mourn and rejoice, but not pass judgment. This is Dehmel's motto of consecretion, his *Weihspruch:*

Klage und juble, Dichter,
Wie du willst;
Das wirkt Seele ins All,
Du bist Gott.
Aber beklage nicht!
Bejuble nicht!

> Nichts!
> Du bist Gottes Werk;
> Brüste dich nicht!

The voluntarism of Schopenhauer and Nietzsche is the pivot of Dehmel's *Weltanschauung.*   Life for our poet is not intellect, but will.   In his *Reminder for his Revered Reader (Denkzettel an den verehrten Leser)*, the prelude to the *Erlösungen*, Dehmel tells us that life's experiences are not born out of thinking; thoughts are but vines that we twine like arabesques about the manifestos of mysterious forces.   Life has no brain and reveals itself to us only as an all animating will.

> Das Leben hat kein Gehirn,
> Verwirrt dir höchstens dein Gehirn,
> Wird dir nur mit Schmerz und Lust
> Als ein beseelender Wille bewusst,
> Der dich unsinnig treibt und lockt,
> Und den zu verdauen, Mensch, unverstockt,
> Mit unsern paar Sinnen für Heid wie Christ
> Die wahre Seelenseligkeit ist.

There is a mystic monism in Dehmel's voluntarism, and expressions like *es brennt, es lechzt, es giert in uns* with the impersonal use of the verb are highly characteristic.   In this respect Dehmel is more akin to Schopenhauer than to Nietzsche. The racial and cosmic aspect of the will is emphasized, the center of volition is not the individual, but the race, the Universe. This is our fate and thus human fate is sublime.

> Was ist dein Los?   Das Menschenlos.
> Das Menschenlos ist immer gross.
> Es ist, o Mensch, der Weltenschoss.

This faith does not produce blind fatalism, passive resignation. To some extent the very sublimity of the conception prevents that; again the individualistic aspect of Dehmel's philosophy looms up: the truly heroic will determines its own fate.

> Das Schicksal will's, nun meinst du: bah,
> Ein Narr, wer eignen Willen schätzt.
> Du Narr, du stehst als Beispiel da,
> Welch Schicksal sich der Wille setzt.

World-will and individual will are the two poles around which all revolves.   They determine the mysterious border be-

tween individual freedom and cosmic necessity. To lift the
veil here would be to solve the mystery of human life and
human fate. Our human prerogative is to become what we are.
Even in erring we can attain this, if we only remain masters of
our endeavor.

> Wenn du auch irrst
> Auf den Bergen des Strebens:
> Nichts ist vergebens,
> Denn du wirst.
> Nur: bleib Herr deines Strebens.
>
> *(Schicksalsworte)*

But to become what we are is not only our prerogative, it is
also our limitation. Compare Goethe's poem *Dämon* (*Urworte.
Orphisch*): "So musst du sein, dir kannst du nicht entfliehen."
We are held within certain fixed limits. Furthermore life is a
winnowing process in which all dross perishes. It is no thing
of evil to the world spirit if the individual perishes, is the message of Hölderlin's poem *Patmos*. In the winnowing process
the lighter corn is thrown to the sparrows; this is Dehmel's
symbol of the development of mankind. We become what we
are:

> Und keine Zeit und keine Macht zerstückelt
> Geprägte Form, die lebend sich entwickelt,

Goethe says, his gaze fixed solely on the elect. Dehmel expresses the same idea in the following poem, but includes the
dross that perishes and does not limit himself to the elect, "die
geprägte Form."

WEN'S TRIFFT

> Schicksal hämmert mit blinden Schlägen,
> Wachs bleibt Wachs, Gold lässt sich prägen,
> Eisen wird Stahl, Glas zerspringt—
> Springt an hundert eiserne Türen,
> Keine Klinke will sich rühren,
> Die den Scherben Rettung bringt.

In us life burns and rages with its creative will, this is an ever
recurring thought of Dehmel. While we pursue our aim, life
seizes us in its tempestuous whirl and forces us to do its bidding.

> Du rennst nach eignem Ziel und Sinn,
> Da kommt das Leben angefahren

Und nimmt dich hin an Hirn und Haaren;
  O nimm es hin.

Noch stürmt dein Herz: ich will, ich will!
Und wilder blutet deine Wunde.
O lass! Vielleicht noch eine Stunde,
  Dann steht es still.

(Zuspruch)

Life is, we see, surrender of our individual will and desires to
the life of the world, a surrender that is not achieved without a
struggle, a struggle that is essential to life. In it we will
gain self-confidence; we will find ourselves if we take our fate as
our own.

Nimm dein Schicksal ganz als deines!
Hinter Sorge, Gram und Grauen
Wirst du dann ein ungemeines
Glück entdecken: Selbstvertrauen.

(Ermutigungen)

In this conflict two possibilities are open to us: Either we
shape life or life shapes us. With this we must figure and
make our choice accordingly.

SELBSTZUCHT

Mensch, du sollst dich selbst erziehen.
Und das wird dir Mancher deuten:
Mensch, du musst dir selbst entfliehen.
Hüte dich vor diesen Leuten!

Rechne ab mit den Gewalten
In dir, um dich. Sie ergeben
Zweierlei: wirst du das Leben,
Wird das Leben dich gestalten?

Mancher hat sich selbst erzogen;
Hat er auch ein Selbst gezüchtet?
Noch hat keiner Gott erflogen,
Der vor Gottes Teufeln flüchtet.

The meaning of this poem seems clear. We are not to
avoid the battle with our passions and natural instincts, but
force them to do our bidding; thus only can we attain our
destined measure of perfection. Our next duty is to gain
clearness of vision as to our aims, desires, purposes, to gain

what Dehmel has called "Zweckbesinnung"; without that we are the slaves of our passions and instincts.

> Wem Zweckbesinnung fehlt,
> Den knechten seine Triebe,

and again:

> Lebe mit Zweck,
> Wirf dich nicht weg,
> Gib dich den andern hin
> Mit eignem Sinn.
>
> (*Zwecksprüche*)

In Dehmel's metaphysical oratorio *Die Vollendung*, the spirit of strength and the spirit of order, desires and duties, contend for the mastery of man.   The spirit of mankind tells his children that the forces that contend in them and for them have borne his pinions aloft and that the battles that they are fighting are lifting him heavenward.   He admonishes his children not to ward off by violence what irrepressibly will come to life, but to listen to the contending powers within the soul, attain clearness of vision and thus gain the mastery.

> Müsst euch versenken
> Tief in den innern Streit,
> Fühlend zerdenken,
> Was in euch schreit.
> Wie's immer wühlt:
> Wenn ihr's zerfühlt,
> Seid ihr befreit.
> Nur wie ihr's auslegt, wird's euch bewusst,
> Wird Heil aus Unheil, Qual aus Lust.
> Denn der Kreislauf der waltenden Mächte
> Will nicht das Gute, will nicht das Schlechte.
> Was euch mit Willen, mit Sehnsucht füllt:
> Wie ihr's begreift, wie ihr's enthüllt,
> Wird es das Falsche, wird es das Rechte.
> Die euch gestalten,
> Die euch erhalten:
> Schaffend zerstörende,
> Tötend gebärende
> Weltgewalten:
> Deckt ihr in eurem
> Ihr Wirken auf,
> Lenkt ihr mit eurem
> Ihren Lauf.

> Die in euch wühlen,
> Alle die Geister,
> Müssen dann fühlen:
> Ich bin ihr Meister!

Here we meet again the new faith that man is God and we see that it strengthens our feeling of responsibility. Even though we grope in darkness we are solely responsible for our deeds and for their consequences, no matter whether we desired the latter or not. This is the stern relentless code that had to come with Darwinism and which Hebbel, George Eliot and George Meredith embodied in their works. Compare also Dehmel's poem *Menschenrecht* in which a human being having rejected the traditional faith wishes also to cast aside all duty and responsibility. Justice and duty rule eternally, even though the supernatural religious belief on which mankind once based them is gone.

> Dein Recht ist deine Kraft—drum bläh dich nicht,
> Du stehst mit deinem Recht vorm Weltgericht.
> "Was? Weltgericht? ein längst entkräftet Wort!"
> Doch setzt die Welt das Richten kräftig fort.
> "Und wenn mein Recht mit Macht dagegen rennt?"
> Kein Recht wird Macht, das seine Pflicht verkennt.
> "Und was ist meine Pflicht, O Weltgewalt?"
> Da sieh Du zu—lacht das Scheusal kalt.
>
> (*Menschenrecht*)

Without the belief in an extra-mundane bearer of light as cheered former ages we grope our way in darkness. On us alone rests the responsibility of every step we may take. Our deeds are ours, ours alone, and ours are the consequences. In us there is seething in turmoil and travail a sea of desires and longings so manifold and various and contradictory that they may blind us to our real will that is one with the world-will. This is the fundamental idea of the poem *Der Wunschgeist*. And in that very power which more than all else unites the individual with the race and from which all life issues—there, strive as we may, we can never attain clearness of vision.

> In allen Tiefen
> Musst du dich prüfen,
> Zu deinen Zielen

> Dich klar zu fühlen.
> Aber die Liebe
> Ist das Trübe.
> (*Leitwort—Aber die Liebe*)

In love's passion, however, the world-will finds utterance in the individual, and clearness of vision, "Zweckbesinnung," is not of prime necessity.   Here man may and must trust his instincts without seeking to fathom them.

> Wem Zweckbesinnung fehlt,
> Den knechten seine Triebe;
> Es sei denn, ihn beherrscht
> Die Herrscherin, die Liebe.
> (*Fürsprüche*)

Love like the sea is "Aufklang der Unendlichkeit" (*Lobgesang*). It overcomes the eternal dualism of I and Thou, and through it we can overcome the barriers of individual existence.

> Lass uns gern einander lauschen,
> Innerst grenzenlos gesellt,
> Sinn und Seele liebreich tauschen,
> So wird kleine grosse Welt.
> (*Fürsprüche*)

Thus finite mortality can attain that rarest of all virtues, tolerance.   Whatever we may strive for, one bond must remain, the desire to understand each other.   The religious tolerance of Lessing's *Nathan* is widened into tolerance of all human endeavor.   Could the greatest gift of the age of rationalism have borne fairer fruit?

> Lasst uns nur ins Blaue schweifen,
> Scheltet nur, wie weit wir's treiben.
> Aber ein Band sollte bleiben,
> Jeden, wie er strebt, begreifen.
> (*Fürsprüche*)

In the chapter on Nietzsche it has been shown that individualism and collectivism do not annul, but supplement each other: the individual can best serve the race through his own maximum of development.   Dehmel was among the first to see the full significance of Nietzsche's teaching and to warn against an ultra-individualistic, purely selfish interpretation.   In his *Nachruf an Nietzsche* the disciple who loved the master comes to

Zarathustra with the question: "Meister, was soll ich tun, dass ich selig werde?" And Zarathustra's gesture and gaze interpret to the youth the command to follow in the footsteps of his Master.

> Zarathustra aber wandte sich
> Und schaute hinter sich,
> Und seine Augen wurden fremd,
> Und gab zur Antwort:
> "Folge mir nach."
> Da ward der Jünger sehend
> Und verstand den Meister:
> Folgte ihm
> Und verliess ihn.

Thus Dehmel illustrates the demand of Nietzsche: "Werde, der du bist." The disciple understands the true significance of Zarathustra's teaching: its supreme unselfishness. He bemoans the fact that Zarathustra came too early to a people that in their selfish way but misunderstood him:

> Seinen Adler sahn sie fliegen,
> Der da heisst
> Der Wille zur Macht
> Über die Kleinen;
> Und seine Schlange nährten sie an ihrer Brust,
> Die Schlange Klugheit.
> Aber seiner Sonne ist ihr Auge blind,
> Die da heisst
> Der Wille zur Macht
> Über den Einen: den Gott Ich.
> Wiedergeburten feiern sie
> Und Wiedertaufen aller Götzen,
> Aber keiner wusste noch
> Sich selber zu befruchten
> Und seinem Samen jubelnd sich zu opfern.

This is Dehmel's, this is Nietzsche's will to sacrifice, to self-sacrifice. Dehmel likes to force the contrast of individualism and collectivism into close proximity, as for example in his song to his son (*Lied an meinen Sohn*). The poet is sitting beside the cradle of his young son; in the springtime night without the storm is raging through the forest, bending the tree tops, stirring and awakening new life, and breaking down with mighty crash what is ripe for destruction. This is a symbol of all life, the eternal triumph of youth over age.   And the father admonishes his son not to heed in later life an aging father's advice of filial duty, but to obey the springtime summons of Nature, the voice of the wind in the tree tops: "Sei Du! Sei Du!" Thus Dehmel makes good his demand of sacrificing one's self to one's posterity, "sich seinem Samen jubelnd zu opfern."   The conflicting claims of the rights of the individual and of mankind and their ultimate solution the poet has compressed into a single stanza under the title *Unterschied*.   The life of Jesus has shown him the way.

> Ein Tropf, wer nie sich selbst gehört,
> Man dankt ihm kaum, wenn er sich plagte;
> Doch Jesus wird als Gott verehrt,
> Weil er sich selbst entsagte.[23]
>
> *(Unterschied)*

Our first duty, then, is to become what we are, to attain the possible maximum individual development, for only thus can we serve humanity.   Otherwise even self-sacrifice is futile.

Dehmel's ethical code, in which the conflict between the individual and the Universe or the race plays such a pivotal part, has found its fullest expression in *Zwei Menschen*, a modern novel in verse, or—as the poet has styled his work—*Roman in Romanzen*.   Raoul Richter, in a truly masterly analysis, calls Dehmel's *Zwei Menschen* the poem in which the modern pantheistic view of life has found its fullest embodiment and names it together with Goethe's *Faust* and Dante's *Divine Comedy*.   This, of course, does not imply any comparison as to the ultimate value of these poems; they belong together merely because they embody more fully than any other the view of life of their respective epochs.   I should like to make one observation however.   It seems an easy matter to adjudge with fairness great works of art of the past, even though they embody a view of life quite foreign to the reader.   One and the same man may, for example, acclaim the beauty of *Job* and *Oidipus* and *De Rerum Natura*, of Calderon and Lucian; the utter dissimilarity of view does not seem to hinder his artistic appreciation.   But how very different is the effect

---

[23] To Dehmel Christ is purely a human being and not a God. Compare his epigram *Christliche Frage*.

> Ist euch der "Heiland der Welt" als Gott nur wert der Verehrung?
> Gilt euch ein menschlicher Gott mehr als ein göttlicher Mensch?

when he meets in modern art a philosophy of life antagonistic
to his own!

The title *Zwei Menschen* could be rendered "Two Lives."
A man and a woman, lovers, seek their unhampered development; law unto themselves alone they burst every restraining
fetter.   Incidental happenings, the lesser experiences of life,
only heighten their ecstatic rapture and they espouse an individualistic pantheism compressed into the formula "Wir
Welt."[24] They are the Gods, they are life, they are the Universe.   But the deeper, the tragic experiences of life, deepen
their insight.   Beside the bier of his first wife, whom he deserted
because she had become alien to his heart and soul, Lukas, the
hero, realizes the terrible Darwinian law that life makes us
murderers: "Wer lebt, hilft töten, ob er will, ob nicht."[25]
And from the grief stricken features of his dead mate there
comes to him that most fundamental ethical precept not to use
another person as a means to an end:

> Aus dem gramvollen Gesicht
> Schlug kalt die Mahnung mir entgegen:
> Keinen zu brauchen, gottgleich allein
> Williges Herz der Welt zu sein.[26]

The true meaning of their faith *Wir Welt* is revealed.   They
are no longer the world, but only a part of the world, filled with
the world-spirit, animated by the world-will, which is not they,
but in which they live and which lives in them.   They see that
life is duty, *Verbindlichkeit*.

> Verbindlichkeit ist Leben,
> Und jeder lebt so völlig, wie er liebt:
> Die Seele will, was sie erfüllt, hingeben,
> Damit die Welt ihr neue Fülle gibt.
> Bei Tag, bei Nacht umschlingt uns wie ein Schatten
> Im kleinsten Kreis die grosse Pflicht:
> Wir alle leben von geborgtem Licht
> Und müssen diese Schuld zurückerstatten.[27]

---

[24] Dehmel. 5, 115.
[25] *Ibid.* 5, 124.
[26] *Ibid.* 5, 124 f.
[27] *Ibid.* 5, 156 f.

Out of this sense of duty, of obligaticn is born the will to sacrifice, to which the poet recurs again and again. In his younger days he had said of himself that he would fain strew his own self with a thousand hands into the world to complete and renew his existence a thousandfold:

> Hier steht Einer, der mit tausend Händen
> Sich selbst wie Saat ins Weltall möchte streuen,
> Um tausendfach sein Dasein zu vollenden,
> Um tausendfach sein Dasein zu erneuen.
> *(Krämerseelen)*

And Dehmel realized the inherently cruel nature of life:

> Lust ist Verschwenden,
> Leben heisst lachen mit blutenden Wunden.
> *(Venus Regina)*

When the World War laid its terrible burden on all, Dehmel defined human happiness as the courage to sacrifice, and he himself, well past fifty, joined the colors as a volunteer.

> Mensch,
> Dein Glück heisst Opfermut.
> *(Lied an Alle)*

What now is the nature of Dehmel's optimism, if one may use a word so consistently abused? His is a faith that affirms life with all its manifold joy and pain and grief. Grief and joy, bliss and pain, circle around life's center with equal blessing, is the opening chord of *Zwei Menschen*.

> Um den Drehpunkt des Lebens kreisen
> Wonne und Schmerz mit gleichem Segen.[28]

The feeling of the eternity of life man owes to suffering; the creative impulse is born from the deepest woe of doubt, pain, and despair. Thus the spirit of mankind speaks in the metaphysical oratorio *Die Vollendung:*

> Lernt, O lernt in der Taufe der Not
> Aller Erlösung innerst Gebot:
> Dem ihr vergebens
> Flucht, dem Leid
> Dankt ihr des Lebens Unendlichkeit:

---

[28] Dehmel. 5, 11.

Nur wer gebannt ist in tägliche Pein,
Will sich erlösen, will ewig sein.
Wenn dann in Zweifels läuternden Fluten,
Wenn dann in Schmerzes stählenden Gluten
Einsam der Mensch zu vergehen meint:
Dann erscheint,
Der zu den Mächten des Alls ihn eint,
Der zu ewiger Wirksamkeit
Sein vergängliches Wirken befreit,
Der im Erschaffenen schaffend sich weist,
Erscheint der Menschheit heiliger Geist.

Amid grief and death and the despair of shattered hopes the poet still hears the unfolding of unborn future possibilities. In Dehmel's sociological poems the reader must needs notice the social conscience, the feeling that each one of us is somehow responsible for the misery of our poorer brothers; compare especially the poems *Bergpsalm* and *Zu eng*. The gloomy picture is relieved by a faith that ultimately a better order will come to the poor and the oppressed; compare the poems *Der Arbeitsmann* and *Vierter Klasse*.

With this faith in life Dehmel has attained even here the haven where beyond these voices there is peace. The best proof is the poem *Befreit*, a husband's farewell to his dying wife.

Du wirst nicht weinen.   Leise, leise
Wirst du lächeln; und wie zur Reise
Geb ich dir Blick und Kuss zurück.
Unsre lieben vier Wände!   Du hast sie bereitet,
Ich habe sie dir zur Welt geweitet—
O Glück!

Dann wirst du heiss meine Hände fassen
Und wirst mir deine Seele lassen,
Lässt unsern Kindern mich zurück.
Du schenktest mir dein ganzes Leben,
Ich will es ihnen wiedergeben—
O Glück!

Es wird sehr bald sein, wir wissen's Beide.
Wir haben einander befreit vom Leide;
So geb ich dich der Welt zurück.
Dann wirst du mir nur noch im Traum erscheinen
Und mich segnen und mit mir weinen—
O Glück!

Is such peace, such serenity of spirit possible in the presence of bitterest affliction?   This might well be asked.   And yet, what did Emerson say when his son Waldo died, the wondrous child, whose silver warble wild outvalued every pulsing sound? His grief, Garnett tells us, was the grief depicted on a Greek funeral monument, beautiful in its subdued intensity.   Emerson wrote: "The innocent and beautiful should not be sourly and gloomily lamented, but with music and fragrant thoughts and sportive recollections."   Thus Emerson could write, thankful for the beauty that had been his.   What does Dehmel mean?   Partly his poem is born of the feeling of unity of all mankind: the wife's rich gift the husband will give to their children.   But this is not all: for this husband and wife life's aim has been achieved, they have freed each other from suffering.   Dehmel himself has told us that this poem has to do with a farewell forever, that a husband is speaking to his dying wife.   He continues: "Leute, die nicht verstehen, Gedichte zu lesen, . . . die allerdings können wohl in der Tat nicht 'verstehen', dass meine Überschrift 'Befreit' ganz einfach auf die Zeile hindeutet: Wir haben einander befreit vom Leide.   Ich meine, mehr Glück kann ein Mensch dem andern doch wohl nicht bieten.   Oder sollte es Menschen geben, die sich nicht einmal 'denken' können, dass eine Seele selbst den erschütterndsten Schmerz leidlos zu ertragen vermag?"[29] Dehmel is not and does not want to be a tragic poet.   He confesses that to him the second part of *Faust* and the still more "untragic" *Peer Gynt* equal all of Shakespeare and Greek tragedy.[30]   Dehmel has walked on to the end of the road that Hebbel set out on.   He has conquered all tragedy, not because he is of a conciliatory nature—to use a word of Goethe—and seeks to evade the tragic elements inherent in life, but because his life principle is the idea of an evolution that leads us upward. His attitude to happiness in life is of a positive nature.   Hebbel's characters seem afraid to seize the joy that is offered them lest they take more than their due.   They but voice their creator's inmost conviction that was born of years of privation and suffering:

---

[29] Quoted by Kunze, 22.
[30] Dehmel.   9, 48.

> Uns dünkt die Freude Altarwein,
> Am Heiligsten ein sünd'ger Raub.

Dehmel defines happiness as man's fairest virtue. It is but the logical outcome of his desire to enrich life and of his faith that life can and will be enriched.

> Glück ist der Menschen schönste Tugend.
> *(Wahrspruch)*

Our poet has not escaped the heart aches that flesh is heir to, his poetry alone were sufficient proof of this, but he retains the joy of existence. He watches a goldfinch flit through a sea of thorny thistles over which the sun is pouring its radiance. This becomes a symbol to him, he wanders on absorbed in quiet reflection:

> Nun will ich stille weitergehn
> Und mir die sonnige Welt besehn,
> Und durch das Leben kreuz und quer,
> Als ob es ohne Stacheln wär',
> Das liebe Leben.
> *(Der Stieglitz)*

BIBLIOGRAPHY

Chamberlain, Houston Stewart. *Goethe.* München, 1913.

Conradi, Hermann. *Gesammelte Schriften.* 3 vols. München, 1911.

Dehmel, Richard. *Gesammelte Werke.* 10 vols. Berlin, 1906-1909. (Dehmel)

Dehmel, Richard. *Schöne wilde Welt.* Berlin. 1913.

Dilthey, Wilhelm. *Das Erlebnis und die Dichtung.* Leipzig. Fourth edition. 1913.

Dünnebier, Hans. *Gottfried Keller und Ludwig Feuerbach.* Zürich. 1913. (Dünnebier)

Eberz, J. *Hölderlins Nachtgesänge. Zeitschrift für vergleichende Literaturgeschichte.* Neue Folge. Bd. XVI, 364 ff. and 449 ff. 1906.

Ermatinger, E. *Gottfried Kellers Leben, Briefe und Tagebücher.* 3 vols. Stuttgart u. Berlin. 1915-1919. (Ermatinger)

Goethe, *Werke. Jubiläums Ausgabe.* 40 vols. Stuttgart u. Berlin. n. d. (J. A.)

Goethe, *Werke. Weimar Ausgabe.* (W. A.)

Grisebach, Eduard. *Der neue Tannhäuser.* (1869) Twentieth edition. Stuttgart. 1902.

Gundolf, Friedrich. *Goethe.* Berlin. 1918. (Gundolf)

Hebbel. *Sämtliche Werke. Tagebücher und Briefe.* (ed. R. M. Werner) 24 vols. Berlin. 1904.

Heine. *Sämtliche Werke* (ed. Ernst Elster). 7 vols. Leipzig u. Wien. n. d. (Heine)

Herrmann, Helene. *Studien zu Heines Romanzero.* Berlin. 1906.

Hölderlin, *Gesammelte Dichtungen.* (Ed. B. Litzmann.) 2 vols. Stuttgart. n. d.

Hölderlin, *Gesammelte Werke.* (Ed. W. Böhm.) 3 vols. Jena. 1907.

Keller, G. *Gesammelte Werke.* 10 vols. Stuttgart u. Berlin.

Kunze, Kurt. *Die Dichtung R. Dehmels als Ausdruck der Zeitseele.* Leipzig. 1914. (Kunze)

Lenau, Nikolaus. *Sämtliche Werke und Briefe.* (Ed. E. Castle.) 6 vols. Leipzig. 1910-1913. (Vol. 6 not published.) (Lenau)

Le Gras, Jules. *Henri Heine, Poete.* Paris. 1897.

Litzmann, C. C. T. *Friedrich Hölderlins Leben. In Briefen von und an Hölderlin.* Berlin. 1890. (Hölderlin, Br.)

Lorm, Hieronymus. *Gedichte.* Dresden. 1886.

Meyer, C. F. *Briefe.* 2 vols. Leipzig. 1908.

Meyer, R. M. *Die deutsche Literatur des neunzehnten Jahrhunderts.* Third edition. Berlin. 1906.

Meyer, R. M. *Nietzsche. Sein Leben und seine Werke.* München. 1913.

Nietzsche, F. *Werke.* 16 vols. Leipzig. 1899 ff. (Nietzsche.)

Nietzsche, F. *Gesammelte Briefe.* 5 vols. Leipzig. 1905-1919. (Nietzsche Br.)

Novalis, *Schriften.* (Ed. J. Minor.) 4 vols. Jena. 1907. (Novalis).

Platen. *Werke.* (Ed. Wolff und Schweizer.) 2 vols. Leipzig u. Wien. n. d.

Platen. *Tagebücher. Auswahl von Erich Petzet.* München. n. d.

Richter, Raoul. *Nietzsche, Sein Leben und sein Werk.* Leipzig. 1903.

Richter, Raoul. *Richard Dehmels "Zwei Menschen" als Epos des modernen Pantheismus. Zeitschrift für moderne Kunstwissenschaft und Ästhetik.* Leipzig. 1908. Pp. 394 ff.

Schönaich-Carolath, Emil V. *Dichtungen.* (1884). Sixth edition. Leipzig. 1903.

Strodtmann, Adolf. *Heines Leben und Werke.* Third edition. Hamburg. 1884. 2 vols. (Strodtmann)

Wilamowitz-Moellendorff, *Ulrich von. Griechische Tragödien.* Vol. 1. Third edition. Berlin. 1901. (Wilamowitz)

Witkop, Philip. *Die neuere deutsche Lyrik.* 2 vols. Leipzig. 1910, 1913.

The above bibliography includes only editions used and works to which this study is directly indebted.